ABILITY-GROUPING
IN PRIMARY SCHOOLS

Critical Guides for
Teacher Educators

You might also like the following books from Critical Publishing.

Beginning Teachers' Learning: Making Experience Count
Katharine Burn, Hazel Hagger and Trevor Mutton
978-1-910391-17-4

Developing Creative and Critical Educational Practitioners
Victoria Door
978-1-909682-37-5

Developing Outstanding Practice in School-based Teacher Education
Edited by Kim Jones and Elizabeth White
978-1-909682-41-2

Dial M for Mentor: Critical Reflections on Mentoring for Coaches, Educators and Trainers
Jonathan Gravells and Susan Wallace
978-1-909330-00-9

How do Expert Primary Classteachers Really Work? A Critical Guide for Teachers, Headteachers and Teacher Educators
Tony Eaude
978-1-909330-01-6

Non-directive Coaching: Attitudes, Approaches and Applications
Bob Thomson
978-1-909330-57-3

Theories of Professional Learning
Carey Philpott
978-1-909682-33-7

Most of our titles are also available in a range of electronic formats. To order please go to our website www.criticalpublishing.com or contact our distributor, NBN International, 10 Thornbury Road, Plymouth PL6 7PP, telephone 01752 202301 or email orders@nbninternational.com.

ABILITY-GROUPING
IN PRIMARY SCHOOLS

Case studies and critical debates

Series Editor: Ian Menter

Critical Guides for
Teacher Educators

Rachel Marks

First published in 2016 by Critical Publishing Ltd

British Library Cataloguing in Publication Data
A CIP record for this book is available from the British Library

ISBN: 978-1-910391-24-2

This book is also available in the following ebook formats:
MOBI: 978-1-910391-25-9
EPUB: 978-1-910391-26-6
Adobe ebook reader: 978-1-910391-27-3

Cover and text design by Greensplash Limited
Project Management by Out of House Publishing
Printed and bound in Great Britain by 4edge Limited, Essex
on FSC approved paper

Critical Publishing
152 Chester Road
Northwich
CW8 4AL
www.criticalpublishing.com

CONTENTS

FOREWORD

It has become something of a cliché to say that those of us involved in teacher education *live in interesting times*. However, such has been the rate of change in many aspects of teacher education in many parts of the world over recent years, that this does actually need to be recognised. Because of the global interest in the quality of teaching and the recognition that teacher learning and the development of teachers play a crucial part in this, politicians and policymakers have shown increasing interest in the nature of teacher preparation. Early in 2013, the British Educational Research Association (BERA) in collaboration with the Royal Society for the Arts (RSA) established an inquiry into the relationship between research and teacher education. The final report from this inquiry was published in 2014 (BERA-RSA, 2014) and sets out a range of findings that include a call for all of those involved – policymakers, practitioners, researchers – '*to exercise leadership amongst their members and partners in promoting the use of evidence, enquiry and evaluation to prioritise the role of research and to make time and resources available for research engagement*' (p 27). One key purpose of this series of *Critical Guides for Teacher Educators* is to provide a resource that will facilitate a concerted move in this direction. The series aims to offer insights for all those with responsibilities in our field to support their critical engagement with practice and policy, through the use of evidence based on research and on experience.

In my experience one of the most difficult challenges for teacher educators is to support their students in *unthinking* some of their taken-for-granted assumptions about teaching and children. Often, among the most significant of these assumptions, is the idea that children have something called a general *ability* that is more or less fixed. What often follows from this assumption is the idea that children are best taught in groups where they share that particular *level of ability* with others.

That it is why it is so important to have Rachel Marks' volume in this series. Drawing very explicitly on her own research that repeatedly enables children's own voices to come through to the reader, she not only debunks erroneous theories about ability, but shows how damaging and destructive these theories can be, by leading to restrictive educational practices. She reviews earlier research in this field. I well remember the impact that the first edition of Rosenthal and Jacobson's *Pygmalion in the Classroom* (1968) had on me and my fellow students when I was undertaking my own primary teacher education in the 1970s. Now, forty years later, this book is full of insights into the impact of ability-based practices and will, I am sure help teacher educators to fulfil one of their most important roles with their learner teachers, that of challenging such thinking. The particular context for Rachel's work is the primary mathematics classroom, but the lessons are there for us all, whatever age ranges and subjects we may be concerned with.

Ian Menter, Series Editor

Emeritus Professor of Teacher Education, University of Oxford

About the series editor

Ian Menter is Emeritus Professor of Teacher Education and was formerly the Director of Professional Programmes at the University of Oxford. He previously worked at the Universities of Glasgow, the West of Scotland, London Metropolitan, the West of England and Gloucestershire. Before that he was a primary school teacher in Bristol, England. His most recent publications include *A Literature Review on Teacher Education for the 21st Century* (Scottish Government) and *A Guide to Practitioner Research in Education* (Sage). His work has also been published in many academic journals.

About the author

Rachel Marks has been a primary school teacher and mathematics co-ordinator in both inner-city and rural schools, teaching pupils across the primary age range. Her research interests include equity issues and the social context of schooling, and she has a PhD in mathematics education in which she explored the implications of ability practices in primary school mathematics. She currently works as a senior lecturer in mathematics education at the University of Brighton, where she teaches across a range of initial teacher education and mathematics specialist courses.

ACKNOWLEDGEMENTS

First and foremost, I would like to thank the anonymous schools, children and teachers for their commitment to the study on which this book is based. The voices of the children and teachers bring the key messages in this book to life and the book would be immensely weaker without their contributions. I also wish to acknowledge the many trainees, teachers, teacher educators and colleagues who have endured listening to me talking about fixed-ability thinking at length and who have encouraged and supported me in disseminating the ideas presented in this book. This book is a development for a teacher and teacher educator audience of my doctoral study and I am indebted to my PhD supervisors: Jeremy Hodgen, Meg Maguire and Mike Askew for their commitment to, and critical perspectives on, my work. I also wish to thank Julia Morris at Critical Publishing and the series editor, Ian Menter, for their supportive feedback throughout the writing process. My doctoral work was funded by a studentship from the Economic and Social Research Council (award number: PTA-031-2006-00387) and I am grateful for this support to conduct the study.

The newspaper article in Chapter 1 is reproduced with permission of Cambridge News.

Finally, sections of this book have previously been published in Forum (Marks, 2013, 2014b) and I wish to acknowledge Symposium Books for their kind permission to reprint this material here.

Setting the scene

4-year-old pupils grouped by ability

A SCHOOL has been criticised for putting children as young as 4 into classes based on their ability.

King's Hedges Primary School, which has three classes at reception level, separates bright pupils in reception from those deemed less academically able.

The Cambridgeshire branch of the National Union of Teachers says "labelling" children as low ability puts a ceiling on ambition that can stay with them for the rest of their education.

But the school says the structure helps maximise the support it can give to those pupils who need it most.

Jon Duveen, secretary of the county's NUT, said ability grouping, which is rare for pupils in the early part of their primary education, assumes that ability is an "unchanging talent".

He added: "It has the inevitable effect of labelling students, especially those deemed to have low ability. This label of 'failure' often stays with the child throughout their education. They cannot do maths, or chemistry, or PE or whatever and this constant labelling has the effect of telling the child that they cannot succeed

GARETH
MCPHERSON
🐦@GarethMcP_CN

and not to aim too high in their ambitions."

A spokesman for the school in Northfield Avenue said its pupils are offered a "personalised curriculum based on their individual needs". A "significant number" of pupils arrive at King's Hedges school with "many complex needs", he said.

The spokesman added: "The school needs to meet those needs as quickly and as cost effectively as possible. In grouping children in this way those who need most support have the greatest access to it.

"If the very high needs children were separated throughout three classes then their access to support would be significantly diluted, less effective and their progress less marked.

"This model has produced some excellent results and our achievement gaps are amongst the smallest in the county.

"Children who arrived at the school having had access to a wide range of experiences were able to

continue to flourish, but those who did not have the skills struggled to make the same amount of progress."

The school said it invites parents and children in to discuss the pupil's needs before grouping, adding that no child has been taken out of reception for that reason.

Kevin Bullock, Fordham Primary's retired headteacher, said he did not introduce streaming or setting, although children needing extra help were often put in groups.

He said: "My take on streaming is if it's well thought out, if it suits the context of the school, it can be effective. But what is more important is teaching and leadership. It's the quality and dedication of the teaching staff that matters, whether there is streaming, setting or whole class teaching. A study of 2,500 children aged 6 and 7 in England by the Institute of Education in London found streaming pupils by ability appeared to entrench educational disadvantage.

Prime Minister David Cameron said earlier this year he would like to see all pupils put in sets for core subjects.

Figure 1.1 Four-year-old pupils grouped by ability
Reproduced with permission of *Cambridge News*

1

This article appeared recently in *Cambridge News* (Mcpherson, 2015). Before reading further in this book, consider the following.

Reflection

» What is your immediate reaction to this article?

» What beliefs underlie your reaction?

» Where do these beliefs stem from?

Core aims of this book

This book is written to support teachers, headteachers and teacher educators in the primary sector to think critically about ability-grouping. The book explores the beliefs and principles widely held in the English education system by engaging with key questions.

» To what extent is this common practice in primary schools?

» Can we reliably identify *bright* children and *less academically able* children? What do these terms mean?

» What are the implications of such practices for teaching and learning?

» How do children feel about such practices?

Ability and ability-grouping in primary education

The use of ability-grouping in primary schools is increasing (Hallam and Parsons, 2013). Policy plays a role in this resurgence, placing teachers in the difficult position of balancing policy directives with the needs of their class. Many approaches taken by teachers to manage an often wide attainment range take the form of some type of ability-grouping.

Grouping by ability requires teachers to hold some notion of what ability is. While it is unlikely that all teachers would give the same definition – this in itself reveals something of the difficulty and complexity of ability-grouping – it is likely their lists would contain a number of similar characteristics of the *bright* or *less able* child. This is not due to teachers seeking to elevate or demonise particular children but to the extraordinary ideology of ability deeply embedded in the English education system perpetuating a belief that individuals come *hard-wired* with a certain level of ability that can – indeed should – be measured and accorded appropriate educational provision.

This ideology of ability is reproduced on a daily basis through the media and popular culture with the language of talent, ability and intelligence commonplace in everyday talk. Immersed in such language and working in educational structures built on notions of selection, ideas of ability become normalised. It is not uncommon, often without shame, to hear an individual assert that they *can't do mathematics*. This raises questions about when and where children begin to engage with such beliefs, resulting in them growing into adults who hold a can/cannot do belief. This book explores what may be happening in primary schools to perpetuate ability language and beliefs.

It is worth noting that ability-grouping, more so in the secondary than primary sector, carries an extensive research base. It is a topic that raises strong and emotive debate and research evidence can be found to support many opinions. It will be clear that I hold a particular position and I do not attempt to disguise that in this book. I do however present the research, both from the published literature and my own study, in a robust and critical manner which I hope will contribute significantly to the on-going debate and open up channels for critical engagement.

You may ask why this topic is important to you. If many other teachers are engaged in ability-grouping practices in primary schools, does it matter? My hope is that the stories in this book – told through the children's voices – will answer that directly. Beyond this we are reaching a saturation point; with the evidence available, it should be possible to move forward, rather than having to repeat the warnings of history. You may wish to reflect on the following from the 1950s and 1960s. The language we use today may be more socially acceptable, but the issues appear alarmingly persistent. The question must be, if doubts were raised – strongly backed by research evidence – at these times, why are we still debating, let alone commonly using, these practices today?

Before 1955 or thereabouts, public confidence in the fairness and accuracy of the [11+] examination rested on the belief that intelligence tests could detect and measure inborn ability. In the middle fifties this belief was strongly challenged by such university teachers as Philip Vernon, Brian Simon, and John Daniels, who demonstrated conclusively that this was not so. None of the tests conceived and tried over the course of sixty years can satisfactorily distinguish natural talent from what has been learned. Heredity and environment are too closely entangled to be closely identified. This means that children from literate homes, with interested and helpful parents, have an enormous advantage over children from culturally poor homes where books are unknown and conversation is either limited or unprintable.

(Pedley, 1963, pp 16–17)

[I]n the homogeneous class of the streamed school the stimulus to learning is reduced ... the slower children appear slower still, accepting the fact that they are too often called 'only B stream', and making less effort than they might ... In the streamed school there is paradoxically another danger, in that, since the children appear to be more on a level, the teacher is tempted to underestimate the diversity of quality and pace of learning which in fact still remain and which must still be catered for.

(DES, 1959, p 69)

3

Key terminology

This book uses some key terms. For clarity these terms are defined below. Throughout this book the term *ability* is presented without quotation marks to aid readability but it is always under question.

> » Ability-grouping: any form of re-grouping on the basis of some idea of ability.
>
> » Setting: children are placed into ability groups between classes for particular subjects; a child could be in different sets for different subjects.
>
> » Streaming: children are placed in the same ability classes for all subjects based on general ability.
>
> » Within-class grouping: children are allocated to table groups within the class for all or some subjects based on general ability or subject-specific ability.
>
> » Mixed-ability: classes are not grouped by ability and in a multi-form entry school each class in a year-group should contain the same range of attainment.

These structures may exist independently or in combination. Children may find themselves further differentiated to table groups (within-class grouping) in sets and streams.

The research study

The evidence presented in this book comes from my longitudinal study across three schools into the use of ability language and practices in primary mathematics classrooms. These schools – Riverside Primary, Parkview Primary and Avenue Primary (all names in this book are pseudonyms) – and their different approaches to ability-grouping are outlined in Chapter 3. The study focused particularly strongly on Parkview Primary and Avenue Primary, which on the surface took very different approaches.

I spent a year observing Year 4 (ages 8–9) and Year 6 (ages 10–11) children in and beyond mathematics lessons. Becoming a constant face in the schools, the children, and to an extent the teachers, took little notice of my presence, allowing me to observe closely how children seemed to experience their lessons and to hear the conversations they engaged in about their learning in the corridors and on the playground. In order to build up a fuller picture of the children's experiences, I focused on three children within each mixed-ability class, top, or bottom set within each year-group at each school – 24 children in total – representing the attainment range in each class or group. Each child, in addition to being observed within and between lessons, was interviewed individually and in groups with conversations about their learning very much dictated by the children. It is these children's voices that appear throughout this book. Data were also obtained from attainment tests and attitudinal questionnaires with all 284 children in the study, although with a purposeful focus on the children's voices, much of this analysis lies outside the scope of this book.

Embedded in the school communities, I had the opportunity to talk informally to many staff as well as interviewing the teachers of the focus children more formally, building up a sense of the schools' ethos, challenges and approaches. This allowed me to critically examine differences in how incidents in the classroom were viewed by teachers and children, putting together the story of ability in the primary school presented across this book.

A focus on mathematics

The decision to focus on mathematics classrooms was purposeful. In primary schools, most children have a mathematics lesson every day, allowing me to build up a wealth of data. Beyond this, mathematics is an interesting case, located at the extreme of our use of ability language. Popular culture plays a role here with the portrayal of real or fictional people in films such as *A Beautiful Mind, The Theory of Everything* and *The Imitation Game* drawing out notions of mathematical ability/talent/genius and often linking these with ideas of intelligence. While it may be okay to say *'I can't do mathematics'* this is less often the case with, for example, reading or writing. Mathematics however is not unique. Similar beliefs can be seen in physical education, music and foreign languages, and notions of general ability (or intelligence) are still readily applied; how often do we hear teachers or parents referring to a *bright child* or a *clever boy or girl*? While most examples in this book refer to mathematics classrooms, the key ideas are transferable and have much to say generally about ability-grouping in the primary school.

The structure of this book

This book provides a broad and critical discussion of ability-grouping in primary schools. A number of questions have been raised in this introduction and the subsequent chapters seek to engage with these, providing a history of ability-grouping in primary education (Chapter 2), an exploration of what ability actually means both to teachers and to children (Chapter 4) and an extended discussion of the overt and nuanced implications of ability language and ability practices in the primary school (Chapters 5–7). At the beginning of each chapter, the critical issues are highlighted. You may wish to reflect on these in light of your own experiences prior to reading each chapter. These critical issues are then returned to at the end of each chapter and addressed in the light of the evidence presented.

IN A **NUTSHELL**

My desire to write this book comes from a series of critical incidents impacting on how I view myself as a learner and on how I came to understand the principles underpinning my teaching. At the age of 12, less than six weeks into the new school year, my French teacher told me to leave the class with the parting words: *'you're not good enough, even for the bottom set'*. I left, never engaging in another French lesson, but taking with me a lasting view of myself as *not good enough*. Then, as a teacher, I engaged in the same language and practices and may, inadvertently, have made children feel very similar. Later, encountering Jo Boaler's work on ability-grouping in secondary mathematics (see, for example, Boaler, 1997a) I was thrown into turmoil as I found myself unable to defend the practices I had engaged in as a teacher. Researching this in the primary context I was struck by one eight-year-old boy, Zackary, telling me he was *just not born clever*. Zackary is just one child, but there are many other *Zackarys* in our primary schools where features of our educational approach allow children at relatively young ages to construct themselves in such derisive terms. This book engages in a critical dialogue with current practices in primary schools exploring what is happening, why it might be happening, and what else could happen. It is intended to prompt thinking and debate and to challenge the status quo. You may wish to begin by reflecting on what brought you to this book.

Reflection

»   What were your experiences of ability-grouping in school?

»   How have these impacted on you as a teacher and learner?

CRITICAL **ISSUES**

- *To what extent is ability-grouping a feature of primary education in England?*
- *What role might policy play in the use of ability-grouping practices in primary schools?*
- *What do we know about the impacts – attitudinal, attainment and economic – of ability-grouping?*

Ability-grouping in England ... and beyond

The use of, and debates around, ability-grouping are nothing new. For almost 100 years ferocious argument has adorned the landscape of education in England as ability-grouping practices have swung between extremes. Embedded in the English ideology and fascination with ideas of ability and intelligence (see Chapter 4) and, as recognised in the 1960s, mirroring the English social system (Pedley, 1963), opponents and advocates have been embroiled in a bitter war, with children's education, and potentially children's future life-chances, at stake. While this book focuses on the education system in England, these phenomena are seen further afield – particularly in the tracking debates in the United States.

This chapter explores the history and impacts of ability-grouping practices in England, with a particular focus on primary education, outlining the current situation and its historical roots. Given the long and complex nature of ability-grouping in England, it is unsurprising to find a plethora of research dating back to the early 1900s although it should be noted that, at primary level, the research is more limited particularly in terms of the relationship between grouping and attainment (Parsons and Hallam, 2014). Rather than rehearse the literature extensively a key overview of understanding from seminal and recent publications, indicating sources you may wish to explore further, is provided.

Changes and developments in ability-grouping practices

The historical nature of our ability ideology and ability-grouping practices is long and complex. The Butler Education Act of 1944 established a need for ability-grouping in primary schools as children worked towards 11 plus examinations (for allocation to grammar or secondary modern schools). Streaming practices were commonplace throughout the 1940s and 1950s (Hallam et al, 2013) with 74 per cent of schools placing children into different classes on the basis of ability by the age of seven (Jackson, 1964).

The inception of comprehensive education and rising concerns about equity, equal opportunities and the negative social consequences of ability-grouping (see, for example, Barker Lunn, 1970; Jackson, 1964) resulted in a dramatic swing towards the use of mixed-ability approaches. During the 1960s and 1970s the use of streaming in primary schools fell to less than three per cent (Lee and Croll, 1995). Mixed-ability practices remained fairly stable until the Education Reform Act (1988) brought about the first national curriculum and paved the way for target-setting, increased accountability and the marketisation of education. Structured ability-grouping began to gain in popularity.

What role does policy play?

From the 1988 Education Reform Act onwards, successive government education policies (across political parties), calling for a rise in standards, appear to have perpetuated the return of structured ability-grouping, in many cases, overtly encouraging such approaches. A commonly cited example of such encouragement was seen in the 1997 White Paper *Excellence in schools* which noted that '*setting should be the norm in secondary schools. In some cases, it is worth considering in primary schools*' (DfEE, 1997, p 38). Even where not so explicitly stated, teachers' readings of policy may have contributed to a rise in ability-grouping. The National Numeracy Framework was implemented in Primary Schools in 1999. While the framework, in itself, did not advocate structured ability-grouping, many schools responded to the Framework's requirement for whole-class teaching by introducing setting in order to reduce the attainment range (Whitburn, 2001).

Support for structured ability-grouping in education policy has continued into the twenty-first century. The 2005 White Paper, *Higher standards, better schools for all, more choice for parents and pupils* (DfES, 2005, p 58), stated that '*Grouping students can help to build motivation, social skills and independence; and most importantly can raise standards because pupils are better engaged in their own learning. We have encouraged schools to use setting since 1997*'. This position, and the assumptions underlying it, continues today, as evident in a recent statement by the former shadow Education Secretary, Tristram Hunt:

Schools should use all the tools at their disposal, including streaming in English and maths where that is necessary. There is nothing wrong in recognising that people are born with different skills and talents. We need to develop all talents, but it is right to recognise that some talents can be stretched further.

(Wintour, 2015)

Policy imperatives such as these appear to have put schools – and increasingly, primary schools – under mounting pressure to adopt structured ability-grouping (Hallam et al, 2013).

The current state of play

It is actually surprisingly difficult to tie down the exact numbers of primary schools currently using different structured ability-groupings. In primary schools, in particular, practices tend to change as children get older with more between-class grouping in the later years. Some schools are restricted in their choice of approach through their size while others circumvent this through mixed-age grouping. Many schools use a combination of approaches, for example, using within-class grouping on top of setting. Further, schools' understanding of the nomenclature may make reporting of practices unreliable.

Despite these difficulties, it is clear that the use of structured ability-grouping is rising. By the end of the twentieth century, while streaming was still virtually non-existent with less than two per cent of primary schools using this approach (Hallam et al, 2003), 60 per cent of junior schools and over one-third of infant schools set for at least one subject (Ofsted, 1998). Of those schools that adopted setting, 96 per cent set for mathematics (ibid). Within-class ability-grouping also rose. At the beginning of the twenty-first century 56 per cent of Reception classes were taught in within-class ability-groups, rising to 72 per cent by Year 2 (Hallam et al, 2003).

Recent evidence on the extent of the use of structured ability-grouping is now coming through from the Millennium Cohort Study, a longitudinal study following 19,000 British children born in 2000–01 through their early childhood and into adult life. This study is beginning to show a shift in approaches. While setting continues to follow an upward trend, streaming now appears to have experienced resurgence. Currently, 16.4 per cent of children in Year 2 (ages 6–7) experience streamed classes (Hallam and Parsons, 2013).

Group allocation

Given the apparent resurgence in structured ability-grouping practices, it is important to take some time to consider how they are enacted and the potential impacts of such approaches. While the research suggests that ability-grouping may be effective where group movement is highly flexible and children's positions continually monitored in light of their changing attainment profiles (Hallam et al, 2013), such experiences appear to be far from common practice. Despite government rhetoric of inclusivity and equity, a lack of fluidity in ability-grouping systems often means that a child's initial group placement is highly significant, giving or restricting access to particular learning opportunities, creating and fixing educational outcomes and life chances at a young age (Bartholomew, 1999).

The creation and fixing of educational opportunities through structured ability-grouping is all the more problematic given copious research indicating the somewhat arbitrary nature of children's allocation to groups. It has been reported since the 1960s that current attainment is just a small part of grouping decisions (Barker Lunn, 1970) with teachers' judgements informing the ability-group a child is placed into. Unconsciously, teachers appear to be biased by stereotypes about different learners, perhaps perpetuated by the constant bombarding of media messages about under-performing groups, resulting in weaker judgements, and hence potentially lower group placement, of some children based on, for example, gender, ethnicity and family income-level (Campbell, 2015). Further research shows that children with special educational needs and disabilities (SEND), long-standing illnesses and those perceived by their parents as having behavioural difficulties are over-represented in bottom sets (Hallam and Parsons, 2014). It is also widely reported that autumn-born children (those who are oldest in any academic year) are substantially over-represented in top groups while summer-born children (the youngest in any academic year) are over-represented in bottom groups. These positions persist and attainment gaps widen as children move through their school careers (Campbell, 2014).

All of these factors point towards the conclusion that ability actually represents something far more complex and multi-faceted in the primary classroom. Structured ability-grouping is far from grouping by current attainment. The disproportionate representation of children from particular social and cultural groups across structured ability-groups means such groupings are, by their very nature, socially divisive (Muijs and Dunne, 2010). Cycles of social and educational disadvantage are created and perpetuated, with disadvantage reinforced across the educational system. Structured ability-grouping potentially legitimises the stigmatisation and differential treatment of others in terms of multiple social characteristics, and it has not been unknown for structured ability-grouping to lead to the perpetuation of bullying (Hallam et al, 2004).

What do we know about teaching and learning in structured ability groups?

The research is quite clear that, *'where structured ability-grouping is implemented, the activities undertaken in the classrooms of high-, middle- and low-ability pupils differ considerably'* (Hallam et al, 2013, p 72). This is perhaps unremarkable given that a core reason cited for implementing structured ability-grouping is to make teaching easier and help teachers in supporting children's individual needs. Indeed, Hallam and Ireson's (2005) survey reported substantial differences in the teaching of different ability-groups, even, surprisingly, when taught by the same teacher.

Teaching to a reference child

It appears that the *Pygmalion Effect*, first reported in a study conducted in the 1960s, continues. Teachers hold different expectations and teach differently when faced with children they perceive to be of different abilities (Rosenthal and Jacobson, 1992; Friedrich et al, 2015). Although each ability-group will be made up of children with a variety of attainments and learning profiles, there appears to be a tendency for teachers to treat the group as homogeneous with children treated as if they are identical in terms of their learning needs (Boaler, 1997b).

Top set children are expected to work at a fast pace, are not expected (or even allowed) to make mistakes or to find work difficult. While expectations may be high, class work, particularly in mathematics, is often procedural with quantity valued over quality or the development of understanding. At secondary level, top sets have been characterised as competitive and, in some cases, anxiety-provoking, particularly for girls (Boaler, 1997a). In contrast, bottom or lower ability-groups have been characterised as having more limited curriculum access with topic omission, repetition and a slow pace. Discussion is discouraged, feedback limited and work often restricted to the completion of worksheets, all indicative of lower expectations, both of work and behaviour (Harlen and Malcolm, 1999).

What is known about the impact of structured ability-grouping?

So far, this chapter has suggested possible disparity in how children are being allocated to structured ability-groups and, once in groups, disparity in the educational approaches and opportunities available to them. Given, too, the reported increase in the use of all forms of structured ability-grouping – particularly in the primary school – it is important to consider what is known about the impacts of these practices on children's education and wider lives.

Attainment outcomes

Policy drives have had a considerable bearing on the increase in the use of structured ability-grouping in England. Given people's fascination with ability and intelligence this seems understandable. Practices align with strongly-held views about potential and talent and it seems rational to expect that an approach designed to allow teachers to focus more deeply on the learning needs of a more limited range of children should have positive outcomes. We are in a position where many school and government policies '*reveal the extent and strength of belief in the setting process as a panacea to underachievement*' (Boaler, 1997b, p 577).

Despite policy imploring the use of structured ability-grouping, the evidence to support this practice as a means of raising attainment is tenuous. Although dated, Slavin's (1987) seminal Best-Evidence Syntheses of 17 studies in primary/elementary education suggests a near zero effect; overall, grouping by ability is unlikely to raise attainment. At secondary level, the use of structured ability-grouping has been associated with widening attainment gaps as pupils in different groups, but crucially with the same initial attainment, perform significantly differently in compulsory examinations (Wiliam and Bartholomew, 2004). The evidence related to primary schools in England is more limited, but a clearer picture is emerging from recent studies. Schools not using structured ability-grouping (ie mixed-ability groups) have achieved significantly better results with low-attaining children in mathematics, without this being at the expense of the attainment of other children (Whitburn, 2001). Evidence from the Millennium Cohort Study suggests some emerging trends:

Those placed in middle or bottom streams do less well in KS1 reading and overall KS1 performance, and children in bottom streams do less well in KS1 mathematics than similar children in mixed ability classes and that those in the top streams do better.

(Parsons and Hallam, 2014, p 580)

Importantly, the authors note that these trends have been seen in Key Stage 1, that is after children have been in school for a relatively short time, again potentially adding to the weight of evidence that structured ability-grouping may create and widen attainment gaps.

Despite government rhetoric, setting and streaming appear to have no evocative impression on overall attainment. The Teaching and Learning Toolkit developed by the Education Endowment Fund (EEF) ranks 35 educational trends and vogues against each other in terms of potential attainment gains. Streaming and setting rank in the penultimate position with an overall average expected gain of minus one month for schools implementing such an approach (EEF, 2015).

Impacts on attitudes

The research concerning the impact of structured ability-grouping on children's attitudes is more equivocal than that for attainment and particularly limited at primary level. There is some evidence to suggest that some of the teaching approaches associated with lower groups have a negative impact on children's attitudes. Indeed, two now famous ethnographic studies of schooling in the 1970s and 1980s (Lacey, 1970; Ball, 1981) painted vivid pictures of the impact of segregating and structuring secondary pupils into ability-groups in creating pro- and anti-school factions.

Generally, studies – albeit small-scale – have argued that the extensive use of structured ability-grouping adversely impacts the attitudes of average and low-ability children (Sukhnandan and Lee, 1998). In mathematics, statistically significant differences are seen between the attitudes of children in high- and low-groups (Hallam and Deathe, 2002) but these are inconsistent and, as mentioned earlier, particular groups of children (such as high-attaining girls) may express different attitudes to their peers. While some children report some positive attitudes towards their group placement, there is a collection of evidence emerging that suggests harmful impacts on attitudes may be experienced at all levels across structured ability-groups (Wilkinson and Penney, 2014).

The longer term impacts of structured ability-grouping

While longitudinal data is scarce, it is not hard to find adults today who experienced streaming at school – and perhaps 11 plus selection/deselection – who will (un)happily regale you with tales of, at least from their perspective, the long-term educational, economic and social implications they and their peers have experienced as a result of the schooling prescribed to them. In light of the upsurge in structured ability-grouping, it is important to listen to these stories.

Studies in England and beyond (eg van Elk et al, 2011) have suggested that negative school experiences as found in low-ability groups and early exposure to structured ability-grouping decrease the likelihood of taking up further training opportunities or of the completion of higher education. Further, evidence recently emerging from a study of data collected from the Program for the International Assessment of Adult Competencies does support anecdotal evidence from adults that 'higher levels of external differentiation (tracking) amplify skills gaps between less- and intermediate-educated adults' (Heisig and Solga, 2015, p 202). With our knowledge that structured ability-grouping widens attainment gaps, even within the first few years of primary school, and our understanding that children rarely move between groups, it is not too farfetched to assert that, potentially, early set placement all but dictates future educational success and that the impacts may persist into adulthood.

IN A **NUTSHELL**

This chapter summarises the current state of play in relation to the use of structured ability-grouping in primary education in England. Evidence suggests that we are seeing a resurgence of such practices, the like of which has not been witnessed since the highly segregated landscape of primary education in the 1940s and 1950s when children, from the age of seven, were prepared for a tripartite secondary education system and to take their expected place in society. While society and its expectations have changed, workplace requirements are different, and ubiquitous selection is no longer a feature of secondary education, government policy continues to pressurise schools into placing children into structured ability-groups, sometimes from the age of four. This comes despite a wealth of evidence that this approach does not have positive outcomes for children's attainment, does not solve concerns over our widening attainment gap, and may have damaging and long-lasting impacts on social cohesion and future economic engagement.

After describing the three schools referred to in this book in terms of their demographics, ethos and approaches to ability-grouping, the following chapters use the children's and teachers' voices to tell a story of how placement into structured ability-groups – which may well be quite arbitrary and reflect bias and stereotypes about particular groups of children – is experienced. For example, how does the stereotypical view that children in top ability groups do not make mistakes play out in the context of primary classrooms today?

REFLECTIONS ON **CRITICAL ISSUES**

- *Structured ability-grouping – in all forms – is a strong feature of primary education in England. Use of such approaches has grown substantially in recent years and is now more rigid and implemented at an earlier age (sometimes as young as four).*

- *At the secondary school level, successive governments have stated that structured ability-grouping should be used. While not mandated, recommendations have been made that it may be appropriate in the primary phase. In an era of accountability, many schools feel under considerable pressure from government to implement structured ability-grouping.*

- *Overall, the use of structured ability-grouping has no, or a slightly negative, impact on attainment. Impacts on attitudes are more equivocal and further research is required. Evidence is emerging that the use of structured ability-grouping in schools may have detrimental consequences persisting into adulthood.*

Introduction

This chapter profiles the three case study schools. As noted in Chapter 1, the study focused strongly on Avenue Primary and Parkview Primary and the contrasts in their practices so these schools are considered here in greater detail.

Riverside, Avenue and Parkview Primaries are all co-educational, mainstream, non-denominational community primary schools serving children aged 3–11 in the boroughs of a large city within, or on the outskirts of, local town centres. Riverside and Parkview Primary are both limited in terms of outdoor spaces with no grassed areas for physical education or play. However, all three schools are within walking distance of urban parkland and river environments. Each school is of above average size (the average primary school currently has 250 children on roll). The socioeconomic status of the schools is substantially different with an above average number of children at Riverside Primary (56 per cent) and Parkview Primary (33 per cent) eligible for free school meals, compared with less than 10 per cent at Avenue Primary. At Riverside and Avenue Primaries the number of children with English as an Additional Language (EAL) is above average with 75 per cent of Riverside Primary children having EAL, while at Parkview Primary the number of EAL children is below average. Each school has an above average number of children with Special Educational Needs and Disabilities (SEND).

Academically, the schools appear different. Table 3.1 outlines the attainment profile of each school. Riverside Primary and Avenue Primary children both achieve highly (securing Level 4 or above in mathematics) against the government's target for primary school leavers at the time of the study. Contextual Value Added scores, a measure of progress across Key Stage 2 which take into account prior attainment and where a score of 100 indicates expected progress (Department for Education, 2008), suggest that at each school children are making at, or in excess of, expected progress.

Table 3.1 Attainment profiles of case study schools

	% of children obtaining Level 4 (or above) in mathematics	Contextual Value Added score
Riverside Primary	88	102.6
Avenue Primary	90	101.1
Parkview Primary	76	99.9

Riverside Primary School

Riverside Primary, with approximately 650 children on roll, serves a multi-racial and cultural community, and an area facing significant social and economic deprivation. The school is surrounded by high-rise, council-owned properties and all children come from this local area. A number of children are refugees and a high proportion of children, when starting the school, are at an early stage in learning English.

Riverside Primary has had a turbulent history with successive changes of leadership leading to instability and perhaps contributing towards historically unsatisfactory external (Ofsted) inspection reports. However, since 2003, the school has experienced stable leadership which has brought with it links with businesses and local universities. The latest inspection report noted that such innovative programmes have significantly impacted on the ethos of, and attainment at, Riverside Primary. The school is now rated as good with outstanding features, and children, given their low starting points, make significant progress.

Teaching and learning at Riverside Primary

At Riverside Primary there are three equal-sized classes in each year. Following the appointment of the new headteacher substantial reorganisation took place. All children are put into sets across Key Stage 2 for mathematics and literacy. Children are assigned to sets based on national curriculum levels (based on the pre-2014 national curriculum). Children are fully aware of how these sets are formed, rehearsing the language of attainment levels so strong in schools today. Further, children are allocated to ability-based table groups within their sets, resulting in the children effectively being double grouped. Tables, seating up to eight children, are numbered from 1 to 4. As with other table-group labels common in primary schools children were fully aware of the meanings of each table:

Table 1, that's clever, really really clever, table 2 is very clever, table 3 is very clever, number 4 is just clever. I'm on 1.

(Tobias, Riverside Primary, Year 4)

At the time of the study, Riverside Primary based its teaching on the requirements of the national curriculum and Primary Framework (this has since been superseded by the 2014 national curriculum). Lessons were strongly practical in nature, with a fast pace and multiple, often competitive, activities.

Avenue Primary School

Avenue Primary is a large, well-resourced three-form entry primary school with just under 700 children on roll. The school is over-subscribed and serves a limited catchment area. It is surrounded by parkland at the end of a road of detached owner-occupied properties. The school is located in a popular commuter area, with many parents in professional occupations.

Upon entering the school, there is an air of professionalism, order and calm. The large Reception area has displays of awards and trophies won by the school, certificates hung in heavy frames and, emphasising the traditional nature of the school, ranked photographs showing the whole-school and various sporting teams. This traditional ethos is also sensed in the behaviour of children, both in lessons and when walking around the school corridors, where children walk quietly in lines and are often picked up by staff for minor misdemeanours.

Avenue Primary holds a strong reputation locally, obtaining outstanding Ofsted inspection reports. The traditional competitive ethos of the school is intensified by being located in a borough with a high proportion of well renowned academically selective and over-subscribed state grammar schools. Secondary school selection tests result in many parents seeking out advantages included paying for private tuition to supplement the education provided by Avenue Primary.

Teaching and learning at Avenue Primary

Avenue Primary has 35 teachers and 40 teaching assistants. Many staff have been at the school for a substantial proportion of their teaching careers although these are balanced by a smaller proportion of younger teachers.

Each year-group at Avenue Primary is divided into three classes. From Year 2 (ages 6–7) these classes are regrouped within years to form four unequal mathematics sets with Set 1 and Set 2 having 30+ children while Sets 3 and 4 have 10–20 children. Children are not put into ability sets for other subjects. Additional staffing is provided by non-class-based members of staff. In the year of this study, Set 1 in Year 4 was taught by the deputy head, Mr Iverson, while the teaching of Set 4 in Year 6 was split between a floating teacher, Mr Leverton, and a Higher Level Teaching Assistant (HLTA). Children are assigned to sets on the basis of attainment tests at the end of Year 1 (ages 5–6) and from Year 2 until the end of Year 6 there is little inter-set movement. Set 1 and 2 children are expected, by the end of Year 6, to achieve or exceed the government targets in national testing. Set 3 children, who are referred to by teachers as the Cusp group, are expected to achieve these targets with additional input. Set 4 children are not expected to achieve these targets and may be disapplied from national testing.

Many Avenue Primary teachers are supportive of ability-grouping, seeing their role to be to increase attainment in external assessment. This sense of needing to impact on attainment appears to be particularly acute as a result of the pressures felt – by teachers, parents and children – to secure places in selective secondary schools. Interestingly, and incongruent with many other teachers, the mathematics subject leader – Mr Fuller – is not a strong advocate for ability-grouping but sees it as necessary given school, curriculum and parental demands. He has tried to move teachers out of their comfort zones, providing, for example, in-service training on teaching approaches and activities designed for a wide attainment range. However, in reality, mixed-attainment approaches are only used, as a last resort, when teachers are forced by staffing issues to take their own classes.

Teaching in mathematics broadly followed the requirements of the national curriculum. Most classrooms are arranged in horseshoe or row arrangements with children facing the front. Usually teachers teach from the front of the classroom with children working individually. Set 4 children in both year groups usually worked with worksheets. Year 4, Set 1 children usually worked through teacher questions handwritten on the board while Year 6 Set 1 children used a combination of interactive whiteboard questions, examination revision books and examples from a Year 7 (ie secondary school level) textbook.

Parkview Primary School

Parkview Primary has 450 children on roll. It serves a wider catchment area than either Riverside or Avenue Primary School and has a more diverse intake. The school is housed in a Victorian building bounded by a railway, housing and roads. Many children live in local council-owned houses, but a substantial minority travel from large detached properties in a popular commuter area further away from the school.

Pinpointing the ethos of Parkview Primary is not simple. The old building lends itself to a feeling of austerity yet this is punctured by the sounds of children and through the display of bright artwork. Although children are encouraged to walk around the school quietly, this is not always observed; combined with the tight enclosed stairways and echoing corridors this means the school rarely seems quiet.

Like Avenue Primary, some children at Parkview Primary transfer to selective state education at 11+. However, these are in a neighbouring borough and heavily over-subscribed. The distance Parkview Primary children are applying from makes a successful application more unlikely. This puts immense pressure on children and their parents with many children undergoing additional private tutoring.

Teaching and learning at Parkview Primary

Parkview Primary has 19 mainstream teachers and a number of specialist SEND teaching staff who also work as teaching assistants. Each year-group is split into two equally sized classes for the majority of their day. These classes are split on a variety of factors common to primary schools including behavioural issues and friendship groupings. Up to and including Year 5 (ages 9–10), children remain in mixed-ability classes for all lessons including mathematics. In Year 6 – noted to be as a result of the pressures of external examinations – children are regrouped into two mathematics sets: a larger top-set and a smaller bottom-set with no movement between sets. Although the sets are officially named as Set 1 and Set 2, the children, and occasionally the teachers, refer to them as the top and bottom sets.

Miss Attwood, the headteacher at Parkview Primary, is a predominant figure within the school. She has a strong belief in mixed-ability teaching expecting this to be the norm up to Year 5. In reality, and unbeknown to Miss Attwood until she quizzed a Year 2 child (Adina, aged 7) as part of my pre-study visit, this was not quite the case:

Miss Attwood: You sit in your classroom groups for maths, don't you?

Adina: No Miss. Miss Mason makes us go and sit in our maths-groups, there's the green-table, the purple-table, the blue-table, the yellow-table and the red-table. The green-table are the best at doing maths, I'm on the red-table, but after break we go back to our normal tables.

(Author's research notes, Parkview Primary)

Up to Year 5, what happens within classes is up to individual teachers and although mixed-ability grouping is encouraged, this is not often the reality experienced by children. In most cases, children are regrouped within the class into ability-based table groups at the beginning at each mathematics lesson. These within-class groups function in similar ways to sets, with limited movement between groups and in some cases, different curricular access. Table groups are labelled – as is common in many primary school classrooms – by a variety of shapes, colours, animals or other objects. In many cases the implications of the labelling (for example from Mopeds to Ferraris) is barely disguised. There were some notable exceptions. For example, Mr Donaldson, who took one of the Year 4 classes, experimented early on with not regrouping for mathematics and instead retained mixed-attainment classroom groupings. What was striking was the early disquiet among the children who appeared to be so conditioned into moving for mathematics that they seemed unsettled by not moving: at one point, one girl was heard whispering to her friend '*he's a silly billy, he's forgotten to move us again*'.

As with the other schools, teaching in mathematics broadly followed the requirements of the national curriculum and Primary Framework. Lessons were heavily influenced by the Numeracy Hour model with clear starter, main activity and usually plenary activities in each lesson although the coherence between these sections was not always clear. Starter activities usually took the form of whole-class games and, as with many aspects of the lessons, could become quite noisy, boisterous and competitive. During lessons there was generally a high degree of interaction between the teacher and children although this was controlled by the teacher in addition to allowed and non-allowed peer interaction. The majority of lessons were taken from online Primary Framework resources and demonstrated via the interactive white board before children completed their own version of similar worksheets. Again, in Year 6, there was a strong focus on preparing for the SATs tests and practising exemplar questions.

IN A **NUTSHELL**

This chapter has briefly described the three schools referred to in this book in terms of their demographics, ethos and approaches to ability-grouping. Read in conjunction with Chapter 1, outlining the study and the focus children, this sets the scene for the rest of the book. The schools' approaches, at face-value, vary significantly from setting across a key stage to flexible, or limited use of within-class ability-grouping. However nuanced – or not – the approaches, these have impacts in terms of how they are enacted and hence how they are experienced by children.

The following chapters explore how children at these schools – particularly at Parkview Primary and Avenue Primary – experienced ability practices. While the children face different approaches to grouping, no two children's experiences of these will be identical and as such, while the similarities within schools are certainly interesting, the fuller story, formed by looking across these schools, gives a broader sense of what is happening with respect to ability-labelling and ability-grouping in primary schools.

REFLECTIONS ON **CRITICAL ISSUES**

- *Reflecting the literature, setting and within-class ability-grouping were widely used across these three case study schools, particularly in mathematics.*

- *How a school chooses to group seems to be dictated more by secondary school selection practices in the schools' catchment areas and by the philosophical stance of the headteacher than by the socioeconomic status or location of the school.*

> ## CRITICAL **ISSUES**
>
> - *What do children think makes people good at mathematics?*
> - *What do children understand by the term ability?*
> - *How do primary teachers use and understand the term ability?*
> - *How does the labelling we use in primary classrooms – such as the blue group – impact on learners and learning?*

Introduction

As a society we, and hence the children in our primary schools, are bombarded with ability predicated language on a daily basis. Television programmes such as *The X Factor* and *Britain's Got Talent* seek to uncover hidden talents while one-off specials – such as *Test the Nation* – tap into society's fascination with intelligence. Newspaper articles featuring child geniuses who have gained early entry to Oxbridge or extensive A* examination passes are commonplace. Free apps – often promoted through social media – suggest they can provide us with our brain-age, brain-strength, and intelligence-quotient, pitting individuals against their friends/followers/contacts and, in some cases, wider society. Underlying all these is the assumption of a real *thing* – often referred to as intelligence or ability – possessed by individuals in varying quantities and relatively impervious to change.

Recently we have seen challenges to the idea of ability as a stable character trait through popular science books exploring brain plasticity and growth (see for example, Dweck, 2012; Syed, 2011). Drawing on advances in neuroscience alongside studies of education, business strategy and sociology, these texts have questioned why we see differences in attainment across a variety of fields from mathematics to music to sporting prowess. However, despite compelling arguments as to the power of individuals to develop their aptitude in various arenas, education in England is still firmly entrenched in the view that ability is fixed.

Difficulties with the term ability

A struggle underlying debates about ability and intelligence is the lack of solid definition. Ability is '*plagued by conceptual problems*', (Howe, 1996, p 40) simultaneously used as a description of what someone can do and as an explanation for why someone can do something. Legend widely reports that Alfred Binet, creator of the intelligence test, when asked to define intelligence replied '*intelligence is what my test measures*'. Multiple terms – ability, standardised test scores, IQ, aptitude, attainment and achievement – are often conflated, muddying attempts at definition. Ability could simply imply current attainment, but as Stobart (2008, p 31) notes, '*the reality is that it shares the assumptions of intelligence testing: that ability is seen as the cause of achievement, rather than a form of it*'.

Ability in education

Despite ability remaining undefined, the term is in widespread use in education. The dominant view in schools is as a fixed determinant of children's future attainment, relatively impervious to change. Through a long history, such beliefs have become elevated to the status of truths through the simple stories they tell and the appeal to a '*basic human need to stratify society*' (Kulik and Kulik, 1982, p 619). Government policy has been based on ideological principles and notions of ability are never far from political debate.

Many teachers, without question, subscribe to the dominant view, with a belief that we can accurately test a child's level of ability and predict their future success. This is despite research (Sternberg, 1998) suggesting that tests are not measuring ability per se but are measuring an individual's current level of attainment. Using such tests to measure *potential* carries many concerns, not least an apparent '*arbitrary*' allocation to groups (Hallam and Toutounji, 1996, p 17). Despite the complexities, ability is the foundation of many forms of classroom organisation. Schools, teachers, parents and children are embedded in a discourse of ability which infiltrates their schooling and wider lives. Given this, it is imperative we understand how children see themselves within this language and the impacts on them as learners.

Children's use of ability language

It was clear early in this study that ability (and associated language: intelligent, clever, smart, dumb, talent, etc) was an everyday component of children's vernacular. This was a language brought up by the children without probing. Perhaps we should not be surprised by this given the extent to which this language surrounds children every day, but it is worth emphasising how strongly children engage with this language, and reflecting on the role of school processes in this engagement.

In everyday talk – particularly so on the playground after results have been given or marked work returned – children discuss ranking. They have no difficulty in labelling how *good* or *bad* they are or in categorising other children as *mathematical* or *not mathematical*. Reflecting Howe's (1997, p 2) suggestion that '*people today have so little hesitation about ranking individuals as being more or less intelligent*', many children appear enthusiastic in positioning their peers. Part of this enthusiasm seems to stem from a rigid and unquestioned belief that this is right. Children voiced an acceptance that '*some people are more clever than other people*' (Catherine, Year 6, Parkview Primary, top set). As in society more generally, ability provides a simple explanation for individual success and failure.

In part, children's use of ability language can be linked with the ability practices they experience. In a similar way to that in which children accept ability as real and happily classify individuals, they see ability-grouping as an appropriate manifestation of this:

Well some people are just, you know, cleverer than other children, that's what decided our groups in Year 3 and it hasn't changed.

(Natalie, Year 6, Avenue Primary, top set)

Natalie epitomises the responses of many children who seek to construct explanations to fit what they see. They hold the belief that individual differences lead directly to group placement and that group placement has not changed as ability is fixed. Whether grouped on ability-based tables within class or into sets, children tend to see themselves as the ability-identifier of their group, building their identities around these labels. When I asked one child, Jessica in Year 4 at Parkview Primary, to tell me about her mathematics lessons, she replied, '*I'm a green person*'. Obviously there was nothing physically *green* about Jessica, but she had taken on the ability-labelling of her table. Similarly, when visiting other primary schools, children as young as six have told me they are: Ferraris, snails, dodecahedrons and mopeds. In the majority of cases the group names barely disguise the assumed ability-level. In a similar vein, many children identified themselves as a national curriculum level, telling me they were a *3C* or that a particular group were the *2As*. Such a phenomenon was described in a study conducted almost 20 years ago (Reay and Wiliam, 1999, p 346) where children came to see themselves '*entirely in terms of the level to which performance in the SATs is ascribed*' and appears if anything, to have intensified in subsequent years. As we move into an era of a new national curriculum and the prospect of assessment without levels, it is essential that educators consider how new practices may be taken on by children and embedded in their identities as learners.

What does ability mean to children?

Given that children readily use the language of ability and take on ability-identifiers, it is worth examining what they believe ability is before considering how these beliefs may impact on learning.

A stark outcome of this study was the consistency in young children's models of ability. While these models could be complex, drawing on multiple ways of thinking, the overriding view of ability was as an innate, genetically determined quality, residing within individuals in specific quantities, with limited possibility for change. Children's models – and we must remember that some of these children were only seven years old – mirrored the models held by secondary school pupils (see for example Hamilton, 2002) and in society more widely.

There was a discernible bias in where children perceived mathematical ability to be located. 70 per cent of children's responses located ability as an internal quality, biologically or genetically determined. At Avenue Primary, where ability-grouping practices were strong, 81 per cent of children's responses located ability as internal. The majority of children modelled ability as something real and located within the individual. When asked what caused high or low mathematical ability children tended to recourse to natural variation, neurological and genetic differences. Children expressed a belief that differences in mathematical ability were apparent from birth '*because you are born with an ability*' (Victoria, Year 4, Avenue Primary, top set). When asked, individually, what made someone good, or otherwise, at mathematics, children repeatedly talked about those who were good at mathematics as being born to be good at mathematics and vice versa:

Wynne: Their brain's bigger. And they're cleverer and better [...] I don't know, it just happens. They were born like that. They were born clever.

Zackary: Some people are just not born clever.

Yolanda: Some people are really good at maths and some people aren't that good at maths. Probably it sometimes runs in the family.

(Year 4, Avenue Primary, bottom set)

Stability in children's thinking about ability

With little movement between ability-groups to challenge children's constructs, and models strongly grounded in biologically determined quantities of ability, children tended to see ability as fixed, relatively unlikely to change. What children *had* was what they *had* and little could be done to change this. Measuring the self-perceptions of ability of all children in this study at the beginning and end of the academic year showed no statistically significant change. Essentially, children's beliefs about their level of ability did not change (for better or worse). These statistical results tie in with the data from interviews with children. Holding a stable model of ability appears to be self-perpetuating with children viewing mathematical ability as an internal force that drives, and to an extent, limits, what they can do. External factors are seen as relatively inconsequential to outcomes with a belief that individuals can only take their attainment to a maximum level determined by internal limits. When asked if they felt they could improve upon their current position, the responses from children were consistent and stark:

Zackary: I think I would not move. I think I would normally stay in the same place. I don't think there's anything I could do to make myself better.

(Year 4, Avenue Primary, bottom set)

Megan: I think I could move a few centimetres further up the line, not far.

(Year 6, Avenue Primary, top set)

Peter: Just about here, not a huge way, well because you can only do so much can't you, it's quite hard.

(Year 6, Avenue Primary, bottom set)

Most children suggested limited room for improvement. They positioned themselves within a hierarchy seen as normal and accepted the place they, their teachers and others gave them. While there were some positive statements from children who felt some improvement could be made, this was tempered by the consistent underpinning theme of immutable limits:

Author: Could anything help you to improve?

Uma: Yes, if we had something like, Mr Iverson, if he explained it out a couple of times and actually came up to me in the lesson and talked it through then I would understand it a bit better.

Author: Could that make you move up higher?

Uma: No, because I have some trouble on a lot of sums with carrying over. I'm way past there in history though, but not in maths, there's this bit [approximately the top 20 per cent of the perceived ability line] I can't get.

(Year 4, Avenue Primary, top set)

Although Uma suggests that intervention from her teacher could lead to improvement, she does not see this as having an impact on her ability which she models as fixed. She talked about a part she would never be able to attain, suggesting a belief in upper boundaries. Extending this, some children suggested that effort cannot overcome predestined limits:

Natalie: I don't think all children can do really well in maths though

Megan: Even if they tried really hard, even if they tried really hard

Natalie: If they tried really hard their best might not be a 5A, but if you have lots of ability and you tried your best then you would do very well in maths. So not all children can do well. [...] If you're determined you might be better but I don't think all children, I don't think, all children can't be, well they could be okay at maths but not really brilliant, because...

Megan: Well you could have people who had lots of ability but they just weren't trying hard enough so they were considered to be not as good but then when they try hard they are really good, but they have to have lots of ability.

(Year 6, Avenue Primary, top set)

Natalie and Megan suggest that you can have ability and not use it but that you cannot move beyond innate limits; effort alone is not enough to achieve success.

Reflection

Before reading further, reflect on Natalie and Megan's model, a model shared by many primary school children.

» What might be the implications for Natalie, Megan, and other children's learning, of holding a model of ability with fixed upper-limits?

>> What classroom experiences might contribute towards their development of a fixed-ability model?

>> To what extent does your model of ability reflect that held by these children?

Teachers' understanding of ability

While the first two questions could be considered hypothetically, the final question asks you to engage with your core beliefs about the possibility for development in all children. If this raised questions or concerns you had not previously considered, you are not alone. It is important to examine teachers' beliefs as these drive the experiences offered in the classroom and impact on learners. Few teachers have the space to reflect on their models and probe their beliefs more deeply. They take on, without question, pervading social views and policy and practice grounded in a fixed-ability ideology. They reproduce practices they were subjected to at school. In many cases, such common classroom practices appear reasonable when married with social beliefs about ability. Hence, beliefs and practices are rarely questioned. Given this I wish to make it abundantly clear that at no stage is this book about blaming teachers or suggesting they are acting maliciously towards particular children. Rather it is about opening up these issues and giving teachers space to critically reflect on, and potentially disrupt, strongly embedded belief systems and associated practices.

It is reasonable to assert from visits to other primary schools, my experience as a primary classteacher, and my work with trainees and teacher educators, that the beliefs of the teachers in this study broadly reflect the beliefs of many teachers in primary schools across the country. These beliefs strongly reflect the social beliefs reflected in children's models. In particular, there was a tendency to take the socially acceptable stance of labelling yourself as *bad at maths*, using this, and its underlying assumptions about biological determination, to assert that some children were *maths people* and some were not, and that to be mathematical requires having a particular type of mind:

I suppose, they, they are just beginning to become aware that some people are more literacy type people and some people are more maths and science type people, they're getting to that age.

(Miss Gundry, Avenue Primary)

Maths is one of those subjects where sometimes they can have a real ability at maths but be really struggling in other subjects, you know you're rarely going to have a child who's an excellent writer but is terrible at everything else whereas sometimes with maths it can definitely be the other way, I mean I've seen kids oh goodness, got 100/100 in the maths SATs tests at the end of Year 6 but they've really struggled to squeeze a level four for their reading and their writing ... Some people have got a very mathematical mind, that is analytical, they're just that kind of learner that lends itself more mathematically.

(Mr Donaldson, Parkview Primary)

Going beyond children's models, teachers may conflate ability, doing well (in mathematics) and intelligence. Often caught in a circular argument, they used intelligence to define ability and ability to define intelligence. This was illustrated by one teacher who, when pushed to explain what ability is, replied:

That's sort of intelligence, I don't know, that's humans. I don't know enough about why humans, you know, I don't know enough about why some people are not as intelligent as other people.

(Miss Gundry, Avenue Primary)

Here, Miss Gundry, as with other teachers, used intelligence interchangeably with ability and with the same assumptions. While acknowledging a limited understanding of the causes of individual differences, her model is firmly grounded in individual difference and the demarcation of this. The intensity with which ability language is used by all school staff, and the fit with social views, goes some way to explain why models and practices go unchallenged. As Povey (2010, p 3) notes, '*labelling by ability, is central to the way learning mathematics is thought about and discussed. The discourse of ability seems so natural that any suggestion that ability is constructed tends to be met with bafflement*'. This was certainly the case with the teachers in this study who, when given space to question practices, found themselves in a sometimes uncomfortable position of questioning long-established practices for the first time:

Why we set in maths and not literacy I don't know either, don't know, no ideas, no, because it's just as big a range of ability ... it's freaked me out now.

(Miss Barton, Parkview Primary)

Immediately obvious in examining teachers' and children's understandings of ability are the resonances between these and social conceptions. Teachers lack spaces to critically reflect on their practices (and underlying beliefs) and hence their practices reproduce the same patterns of inclusion and exclusion that the teachers themselves were subject to.

Implications for learners and learning

In the following chapters, I examine how teachers' and children's beliefs in fixed-ability, with assumed attainment limits, play out in the classroom and wider school. Prior to that, the reader may find it useful to engage with a classroom incident and begin to reflect on where we see ability-beliefs – particularly limits to attainment – surfacing through classroom language and practices.

Ability perceptions and opportunity to learn – a case study

In developing their understanding of place value, the children (Year 4, Avenue Primary, bottom set) are asked to count backwards, in tens, from different starting numbers, exploring which digits change. The teacher, Mrs Jerrett, challenges the children to start from different numbers, with these numbers carefully selected to ensure the children do not pass through any hundreds boundaries (for example stopping the counting before the children moved from 406 to 396):

Mrs Jerrett: Right Charlie, I want you to start from…

Charlie: [interrupts the teacher]… Two thousand, six hundred and ninety eight

Mrs Jerrett: Oh no, we'll keep it to the hundreds, I think 571

Charlie: I want to do thousands. 2698, 2688, 2678, 2668…

Mrs Jerrett: No, that's too difficult.

Following this, Mrs Jerrett started with another three-digit number with the whole class. Charlie continued to mutter the sequence under his breath, counting backwards in tens and correctly passing through the hundreds boundary from 2608 to 2598.

How could we view this incident in terms of fixed-ability beliefs? What are the implications for Charlie and other learners? Mrs Jerrett imposes a limit on the whole class in terms of avoiding the hundreds boundary and on Charlie specifically, verbalising that thousands are *too difficult*. Mathematically, the only difference between Charlie's starting number and the three-digit starting numbers is the need to recognise that the thousands digit, in addition to the hundreds digit, does not alter. Conceptually, the mathematics is the same whether working with thousands or hundreds, yet the use of smaller numbers with children assumed to be low ability is commonly seen in schools. As was the case with Mrs Jerrett, a common justification for this is that smaller numbers are less frightening and there is a desire to protect children – children who it is assumed have quite significant limits on how far they can take their mathematical learning – from *scary* or difficult mathematics. However, such actions may carry deeper implications. Here I outline three.

1. These children are not given the opportunity to explore our number system more deeply; they do not experience the patterning of the place-value system, and hence may have a fragmentary understanding of number, limiting later exploratory mathematical work. Charlie's muttering indicates he has a developed understanding of the patterning involved in the number system, but his opportunities to work with this are limited by low expectations potentially driven by fixed-ability thinking.

2. Young children are fascinated by large numbers; to restrict opportunities to play with and explore these may inadvertently impact on children's attitudes towards mathematics.

3. Introducing artificial limits to learning – stating that something is too difficult for a particular group of children – reinforces these children's models of ability and the belief that there are pre-set limits to what they can achieve.

IN A **NUTSHELL**

This chapter has explored how children form understandings of mathematical ability that are likely to be carried into and beyond secondary mathematics. Children's models of ability tend to mirror the language they encounter in their social worlds. The overriding view of mathematical ability is as innate, biologically determined, and residing within individuals in specific quantities. Many children believe attainment has a set limit and there is little they can do to change this. Primary classteachers, reproducing experiences they had in school and again mirroring social language, are engaged in a vicious cycle perpetuating fixed-ability beliefs as normal and related school processes as common sense. These processes, such as ability-grouping, construct children as mathematically able or not. Teachers are not engaged in these processes out of malice but because they have neither the space nor reason to question such commonplace language and practices. However, fixed-ability beliefs impact on learning, limiting children's engagement with the feeling that effort is futile and limiting the opportunities provided by teachers. As such, it is important to find spaces to reflect on our role in children's ability understandings as well as on the beliefs we hold and the impact of these on practices.

REFLECTIONS ON **CRITICAL ISSUES**

- *Children develop an understanding of ability based on the language they hear around them. Many children think, and accept, that some people are born good at mathematics, while others are not.*

- *Holding a fixed-ability model, children tend to understand ability as the limit of attainment.*

- *Primary teachers have similar models to children, reflecting social beliefs and reproducing the language and practices they experienced as children.*

- *Processes arising out of fixed-ability models, such as ability-group labelling, may reinforce children's beliefs in attainment limits, limit opportunities to learn, and restrict engagement.*

CHAPTER 5 | ABILITY-GROUPING AND PEDAGOGIC PRACTICES

CRITICAL ISSUES

- *How does fixed-ability thinking influence teaching and learning in the primary school?*
- *What are some of the key characteristics of different ability-groups in the primary school?*
- *What implications might ability-grouped teaching have for children's learning?*

Introduction

The previous chapter examined the fixed and deterministic views of ability – particularly mathematical ability – held by children and teachers. This chapter looks at how these belief systems play out in the classroom: what does the classroom look like under a fixed-ability mindset and what are the outcomes of such teaching for children's learning? Much has been written about ability-grouped classrooms at the secondary school level but this has been relatively unexplored at the primary level. You may notice the similarity between the experiences discussed here in the primary setting and the experiences discussed in the literature pertaining to secondary schools. The potential implications of imposing a form of educational organisation from the secondary environment into the primary school are discussed further in Chapter 6.

In line with evidence from other primary schools, both Avenue Primary and Parkview Primary created uneven sets with more children in the top sets (see Table 5.1).

Teachers talked about having fewer children in the lower sets as supportive. You may wish to consider why this view exists and the implications – both positive and negative – for children in a small teaching group. What is interesting to note is that although teachers talked supportively about creating smaller groups for lower sets, the resultant implication of having larger groups for higher sets was not considered. Further strategic organisation was apparent in the allocation of teachers to each set. Far from being random, each school made decisions about where to place teachers and were quite open about making choices most likely to maximise outcomes (for the school, if not for individual children):

Usually we put the strongest teacher in the Cusp group [Set 3] or in the most able group [Set 1], they're the main two.

(Mr Iverson, Avenue Primary)

Table 5.1 Composition of mathematics sets at Avenue Primary and Parkview Primary

School	Year	Set	Number of children
Avenue Primary	4	1 (top)	30
		2	30
		3	19
		4	11
	6	1	31
		2	31
		3	17
		4	9
Parkview Primary	6	1	35
		2	19

A further imbalance in the formation of sets could be seen in the allocation of boys and girls to each set. In line with previous research going back to the streaming studies of the 1960s, boys were overrepresented in the top and bottom sets with boys forming two-thirds of the bottom sets at Avenue Primary. This overrepresentation of boys may account in part for the strong behavioural focus of the bottom sets, one of the themes discussed in this chapter.

Teaching and learning in top sets

Top set teaching and learning strongly reflected what is known about top set teaching in secondary mathematics. Namely, this was an environment characterised by procedural and rote learning at a significant pace, competition between children and, for some – particularly girls – limited opportunities to understand the underlying mathematics and a high degree of anxiety (Boaler, 1997a). These features are discussed below and in Chapter 7.

Procedural and rote learning

Many top set mathematics lessons had a similar feel, being focussed on procedural learning – the application of methods and algorithms – rather than on learning for understanding. Children (sat in rows in all the top sets) were taught methods by the teacher from the front of the classroom and were expected to apply these methods without questioning, or developing an understanding of, the underlying mathematical principles. The predominant focus of such lessons was on the children attaining the correct answer. On no occasion during the observations of top sets were children seen to ask *why*; they appeared to accept a view of mathematics as methods, and worked through the memorisation and application of these without question. For these children, to be mathematical was to be disciplined and methodical in the approach to the taught methods. This, in many ways, reflects ideas of mathematical ability discussed in the previous chapter.

Top set children were expected to display ease in the application of methods. In some cases it appeared that a focus on understanding was included within the lesson, yet this often proved to be superficial. For instance, in the Year 4 top set at Avenue Primary, children were often asked what different terms, for instance partitioning (meaning to split a number into two or more numbers, usually tens and ones), meant, yet there was a shift from *what* to *how* in children's responses. *How* answers were accepted by the teacher and appeared to be the sought response, with the *what* and *why* left unanswered. Such a view of, and approach to, mathematics resulted in inefficient methods of working that would not support children outside of the mathematics classroom. Children were observed applying methods absent of thought, turning to standard algorithms without considering their appropriateness:

Many of the questions, despite being mental mathematics, are approached from the perspective of standard algorithms, even if this wouldn't be how they were done in real life: The question reads £100 – £17.47. The teacher gets the children to partition £17.47 into £17, 40p and 7p. Each part is then taken away. The same is repeated for 1000–989.

(Author's research notes, Avenue Primary, Year 4, top set)

Sticking rigidly with a given method rather than taking the time to explore and discuss possible approaches misses important opportunities to develop children's mathematical fluency or a feel for – or comfortableness with – number. This potentially divorces the mathematics in the classroom from mathematics outside the classroom and leads to questions about the purpose of procedural teaching. Many children, when questioned about their work, were unable to identify mistakes in the procedural application or to think about why they were doing something beyond saying '*that's what Miss Barton said to do*' (Parkview Primary, Year 6, top set). As in Boaler's (1997a) study of secondary mathematics, the most successful children were those who could (would) follow rules and apply methods without question, often at the expense of developing flexibility and independent thought.

Pace and competition

Top set lessons were often dominated by a fast pace and a race towards producing as many answers as possible. Speed appeared to be highly valued. This approach impacted on children's attitudes, with a competitive environment leading to children being self-interested rather than concerned with working co-operatively (see Chapter 7). Children were given regular time prompts and were praised for responding to this, sometimes regardless of the content of their work. In lessons, teachers highlighted speed as a positive behaviour:

The teacher states for the whole class to hear: "I notice that Simon is on question six already". At this, another child says that he is on question seven, another that he has finished, and a competitive discussion erupts.

(Avenue Primary, Year 4, top set)

During the lesson, children on the top table were having a race with each other to see who could complete the most questions. When the teacher came to see what they were doing, they explained that they were racing, and without looking at their work, the teacher said that this was good.

(Parkview Primary, Year 6, top set)

It is particularly telling that the teacher did not check the content of the children's work. They had used an inefficient strategy, yet assumptions of speed as understanding resulted in a missed opportunity for discussion of efficient methods. Praise instead was given to the behaviour – racing – which the children drew her attention to. Children were encouraged to work quickly, over, perhaps, working precisely, with a competitive atmosphere encouraged. Incidents such as these were common, with the work of one child highlighted as an example for others to follow. However, it was often not the mathematics at the centre of the praise, but a learning behaviour, in this case, speed of working. In some cases it appeared that the teacher deliberately chose a particular child, ensuring discussion did occur, adding pressure to work quickly.

Pace, as a feature of top sets, was heightened through teachers' practices, with a lack of wait time after asking questions. Quick, concise responses were expected. Where children appeared to be thinking about their answers, teachers sometimes redirected the question to another child. Top set classroom language was dominated by speed: whizzing on, working quicker, and storming ahead. Such a dominance of pace is likely to impact on the types of mathematics and ways of working made available to children, perhaps limiting opportunities for more creative mathematics or problem-solving approaches.

Teaching and learning in bottom sets

Teachers often talked about wanting to protect the lowest attainers from what they regarded as *frightening* mathematics (such as numbers in the thousands). Enacted from a position of care, teachers used practices with the well-meant intention of ensuring children in the lowest sets experienced success in the mathematics classroom. Lessons in these sets were predominantly built on concrete work, using cubes to complete tasks with small numbers. Logically it is understandable how this approach might be thought of as supportive, yet it had a number of unintended impacts, restricting children's mathematical development.

A limited pedagogy

When asked to describe their mathematics lessons, Samuel, in the bottom set in Year 6 at Avenue Primary noted that: *'with us, everyone is asleep'*. This response was not atypical. At Parkview Primary the bottom set Year 6 children also referred to boredom and falling asleep:

Delyth: … boring

Emily: Sometimes

Finn: It's just [makes 'snoring' noise]

(Parkview Primary, Year 6, bottom set)

While children in other sets may have held similar feelings about mathematics lessons, there appears to be something particular about bottom set lessons that led to these children verbalising such feelings and such an apparent mismatch between children's experiences and teachers' intentions. A potential catalyst for these feelings may be the level and type of tasks made available to the children and the accompanying teaching methods. As illustrated in the case study of Charlie in Chapter 4, teachers felt that children in the bottom sets could only cope with small numbers. While the children showed a curiosity and sense of excitement about larger numbers, something which may have provided an opportunity for mathematical engagement and discussion, the teachers were very quick to stick rigidly with the use of small numbers, unintentionally erecting barriers to children's mathematical development.

Teaching methods in the bottom sets were driven by assumptions about fixed-ability and appropriate learning approaches for low-attaining children. Unlike other sets, bottom sets did not receive a curriculum based on the Primary Framework (the national framework for the content and methods of teaching mathematics in place at the time of the study). Instead, work in the bottom sets often took the form of low-level repetitive worksheets completed on an individual basis. Teachers rationalised the low-levelness stating that it allowed children to experience success and boosted self-esteem. However, watching Year 6 children (ages 10–11) being handed worksheets clearly marked as Year 1 (ages 5–6) only seemed to demoralise and antagonise and may, for some children, have led to behavioural responses which served to support teachers' fixed-ability beliefs.

Concrete approaches

Reflecting teachers' beliefs about mathematical ability – particularly that low-ability children required a kinaesthetic approach – and supporting their desire to protect these children from frightening numbers, teachers of the lowest sets commonly expected children to work through each of their low-level questions using cubes or counters. Such an approach has been reported in the literature as commonplace in lower sets at secondary level (Oakes, 1982) and many trainee teachers report seeing mathematical resources only used with the lowest attainers in their placement schools. While the appropriate use of manipulatives can support all children's learning, the literature suggests that continuously using small numbers and cubes forces children into using less sophisticated counting models – counting out cubes and counting all the cubes together – rather than having the opportunity to learn to work, for instance, with derived facts. This leads to children doing more, if unhelpful, mathematics, potentially restricting their mathematical development (Gray and Tall, 1994).

Given that many teachers assigned to bottom sets are themselves under-confident in mathematics, it is perhaps unsurprising that the implications of a solely concrete based approach were not explored or that these teachers did not have alternative approaches and ways of responding. This was illustrated in a lesson where a child could respond to the task without the use of cubes but rather than using this and extending the child's learning, the teacher responded in terms of seeing anything but a cubes approach as wrong and requiring the repetition of the task in the *correct* manner:

Concrete approaches to learning – a case study

Zackary is working on the question '57 + 32 ='. He has set this out vertically. The children are expected to use cubes to support them with each stage mixing a traditional algorithm with using manipulatives. However, Zackary seems confident that he knows 7 + 2 and 5 + 3 (applying the method taught by the teacher) without the need for cubes so he works through the questions fairly quickly. When he excitedly tells the teacher he has finished and admits not using the cubes, he is told to go back and re-do each one with the cubes. Unhappy with the response, Zackary does not check his answers but instead uses his cubes to build a light-sabre and silently attack a child sitting across the classroom. The teacher notices this behaviour and chastises this, saying '*that is not what we use the cubes for*' and tells him that he needs to get on with his work.

(Avenue Primary, Year 4, bottom set)

Limited discussion and a behavioural focus

While teachers create small groups with the belief that this is supportive, in a size-restricted group there is a tendency towards teacher–child rather than peer–peer interactions. The '*poor interactive dynamics*' found in secondary school research (Pedder, 2006, p 228) were seen in the bottom sets in this study leading to an over-reliance on the teacher for the *correct* answer, possibly restricting children's development of self-help strategies and supporting a view of mathematics dominated by achieving one correct solution. In addition, many teachers conflate notions of low-ability with poor behaviour, resulting in a high level of behavioural reprimands in lower sets:

[T]rack levels differed primarily in the amount of class time teachers and students reported was spent on behavior and discipline and in students' perceptions of their teachers as concerned or as punitive … Students in low-track classes saw their teachers as the most punitive and least concerned about them. Teachers in these classes spent the most class time of any of the groups of teachers on student behavior and discipline.

(Oakes, 1982, pp 114–16)

Oakes' analysis showed that teachers were spending more time engaged in behavioural interactions in lower sets. An implication of the high behavioural focus and small group size of bottom sets was that mathematical discussion was limited. Mathematical discussion was not always highly evident in the fast-paced top sets either, but the lack of such talk and the reasons for it appeared to be different in lower sets making it even less likely to occur.

Beliefs about poor behaviour resulted in erroneous assumptions being made about the causes of any disruption; this was immediately thought to have a behavioural cause, one which needed to be controlled, rather than there being a possibility of it having a mathematical basis. Any talk, even overtly mathematical talk, was interpreted through a behavioural lens, resulting in behavioural reprimands, stifling mathematical discussion and resulting in missed opportunities for mathematical engagement:

Restricting discussion – a case study

The class are completing a worksheet on division by two (ie 10 ÷ 2 =). They are expected to work individually and are using cubes to get the answers before completing these on their sheets. Working on the question 18 ÷ 2 = Samuel is taking 18 cubes and placing them into groups of two, counting the nine groups produced to obtain his answer.

Samuel is sitting close to his friend Saul. He notices that Saul, working on the same question, has taken his 18 cubes and split them into two equal groups, counting up the nine cubes in each group to obtain his answer.

Samuel tells Saul that he is doing it wrong, which leads to an animated and mathematically interesting discussion between the boys as they compare their methods and answers, attempting to understand why they have the same answers from different methods. Very quickly, their discussion is interrupted by the teacher who admonishes them for the noise they are making and tells them they must work individually.

(Avenue Primary, Year 6, bottom set)

Both Samuel's and Saul's approaches are correct, although they reflect different models: grouping and sharing. The behavioural focus of the bottom set may have led the teacher to immediately respond in behavioural terms rather than consider that there may be a mathematical basis to the discussion. As such the opportunity for an interesting mathematical discussion on models of division was lost, an experience which when repeated across multiple lessons restricts mathematical engagement and learning for children and may, along with other bottom set teaching practices, result in restricted attainment.

Outcomes of setting

The use of structured ability-grouping practices – and the fixed-ability mindset they are rooted in – appears to limit mathematics teaching and learning opportunities in different ways. Children allocated to the top sets were adept at applying methods and producing pages of correct answers but their wider mathematical development appears to be more restricted and it is worth considering the longer-term implications of a mathematical diet comprised of rote and procedural learning, pace and a competitive environment. For bottom set children, some of their teaching and learning experiences, for instance a heavy reliance on answers rather than understanding, may be similar to the experiences of children in top sets, but these experiences are intensified by the perceived need for high levels of control both over behavioural factors and the actual mathematics the children are exposed to.

Academically, the impact of these learning experiences is complex. As discussed in Chapter 2, research on the academic outcomes of the use, or otherwise, of structured ability-grouping is somewhat tenuous. At the primary school level, evidence is quite limited. In Year 6, those children in the top set at Avenue Primary made mathematical age gains in line with age expectations, ie in the ten months between the administration of the pre- and post-tests they made an average mathematical age gain of ten months. While all these children exceeded the government target in the end of primary school mathematics tests, and were certainly adept at applying procedures and following rules, their mediocre mathematical age gain – given these children are identified as *mathematically able* – may be an indication of the types of teaching and learning they have been exposed to. In the same ten-month time period, children in the bottom set made an average mathematical age gain of seven months, widening the attainment gap between themselves and other Year 6 children at the same school. Given their impoverished mathematical diet this is perhaps unsurprising and these results fit the wider literature on a growing attainment gap between high and low achieving children.

Further issues

The increasing attainment gap is more complex than simply being an artefact of the children's mathematics teaching and learning experiences. There is evidence that wider practices from the secondary environment are infiltrating the primary environment – possibly justified by fixed-ability thinking – and impacting on children's experiences.

> » Educational triage: While top and bottom set children made mediocre math-ematics attainment gains, those children in Set 3 made an average gain of over one year and four months in the same ten-month time period. In order to obtain the best possible league table outcomes for the school, teachers used beliefs

about ability and potential to justify directing resources at Set 3 who all went on to achieve the government target for the end of primary school. However, directing resources in this way resulted in other sets potentially receiving a more impoverished experience. Fixed-ability thinking allowed the school to justify taking this approach; under such a belief system bottom set children did not have the potential to achieve and top set children were already achieving at the required level, so it was deemed sensible to direct limited resources where they would have most impact (see Marks, 2014a, for further discussion of the process of educational triage and its impact at Avenue Primary).

» Restricted futures: The mathematical diet of bottom set children resulting from fixed-ability beliefs, behavioural beliefs and the unintended consequences of allocating resources to other children through educational triage means that bottom set children do not have access to the same curriculum as others, restricting possibilities for movement between sets. Extending the secondary school research discussed in Chapter 2, it appears that some primary school children are also having opportunities curtailed and their futures restricted at a very early age.

IN A **NUTSHELL**

The style and characteristics of the set lessons reflected many of the characteristics of set secondary school mathematics lessons. Top set lessons, focussing on procedural learning rather than on learning for understanding, were fast paced, with children racing to produce as many answers as possible. Bottom set lessons, drawing on the perceived need for a kinaesthetic approach, had a heavy reliance on the use of manipulatives. There was greater focus on behaviour and a higher incidence of behavioural reprimands than in top sets. Lessons were slow-paced, focussing on repetitive practices and small numbers, hence widening the attainment gap. However, it is important to note that in many cases, teachers believed they were acting in the best interests of the children, performing caring roles in ensuring children were not frightened or distressed by the mathematics.

The often unintended restriction of mathematical learning opportunities for many top and bottom set children resulted in mediocre attainment gains. However, the outcomes of structured ability-grouping go further: Chapter 6 examines some of the nuanced implications of bringing setting – essentially a secondary school pedagogic practice – into the primary school, while Chapter 7 engages with children's experiences of ability-grouping as they work to develop peer relationships in an environment that may run counter to this and under a belief system suggesting to children that '*you can only do so much can't you?*' (Peter, Avenue Primary, Year 6, bottom set).

REFLECTIONS ON **CRITICAL ISSUES**

- *Teachers appear to make choices about pedagogic methods based on widespread beliefs about mathematical ability, using ideas about potential to justify the allocation of resources.*

- *Structured ability-groups in the primary school strongly resemble structured ability-groups in the secondary school. Top groups are characterised by procedural learning in a fast-paced competitive environment, while bottom groups often work on low-level repetitive tasks at a slow pace supported by manipulatives.*

- *Both top and bottom set pedagogic practices restrict – for different reasons – collaborative working, mathematical discussion and, to an extent, access to rich problem-solving activities.*

CRITICAL **ISSUES**

- *What are some of the wider impacts of ability-grouping specific to primary schools?*

- *To what extent can the primary school environment accommodate between-class ability-grouping?*

- *How does the use of ability-grouping impact on the traditional pastoral role of the primary school teacher?*

Introduction

The previous chapter explored the impacts of ability-grouping in primary schools on teaching practices and on children's learning. Much published research on ability-grouping is centred on three areas: group allocation, attainment and attitude. Rarely examined, but pertinent to the primary environment, are the more hidden consequences of ability-grouping. Embedding ability-grouping – particularly setting – creates structural conflict, fundamentally changing the nature of primary schools through the imposition of secondary practices and cultures and the loss of pastoral care. This chapter examines the hidden implications for primary teachers and children of taking on secondary school roles within the primary school environment. It highlights the nuanced impacts of the use of setting, including impacts on the learning environment, the shift towards subject-based thinking and the erosion of the pastoral-centred holistic ethos of primary education.

Pastoral care and the traditional ethos of the primary school

The traditional image of the primary school in England is one organised on a classroom and classteacher system with one generalist teacher per class, teaching the children for most of the day (perhaps with the exception of specialist input for subjects such as music and foreign languages). This structure sees teachers involved with their children at many non-subject based times from routine administration while taking the register, through accompanying their class to assemblies, maintaining vigilance on playground duty, and organising after-school activities. England is unique in terms of its approach to pastoral care, with the child's welfare central to the role of the primary school teacher (Broadfoot et al, 1987).

This position of care is an important consideration when examining ability-grouping which has the potential to fracture the traditional role. Setting exposes a rupture between the physical set up of the primary school, designed for each class to stay within its base for the majority of the day, and the children's movements arising from relocation to group teaching rooms. The implications of children's movement away from their classteacher for setted lessons were evident both at Avenue Primary and Parkview Primary.

At both schools, particularly where children were set for the first lesson of the day, the beginning of the day did not resemble the traditional beginning of a primary school day but a rushed and stressful time as teachers attempted to settle the class and deal with daily administration tasks before children moved to other classrooms. The use of setting imposes a rigid timetable where setted lessons must start and finish at a specified time. In the absence of setting, primary teachers can make decisions to rearrange their timetable in response to emerging needs. If the class are unsettled due to an external incident the classteacher can make time to address this. If a child arrives at school in a distressed state, this can be acted on immediately. However, where setting imposes an urgency to send children to other teachers and a new group of children are arriving outside the classroom-door, the space for pastoral care is restricted. Children may be sent to set lessons in distressed states without communication of this to the set teacher and, at times, find it difficult to engage as they are struggling to make sense of other events: events which may seem trivial, such as falling out with friends, but which impact significantly on young children's engagement.

Displacement and disruption

Setting, which, even in the absence of bells, must happen at rigidly controlled times, displaces children and causes disruption to established teacher–child and child–child relationships. Children are moved away from their peers and from the classteacher with whom they have developed a relationship. It is important to remember that children's class and external relationships still remain, even if momentarily broken for the duration of a set lesson, yet setting often fails to account for the relationships children bring, with these apparently ignored when a child enters a set classroom. The strength and impact of these forgotten relationships was exemplified when children were asked about how they felt during set mathematics lessons. Much of what children talked about related to incidents and relationships outside of, but which impacted on what happened in, the mathematics classroom:

If it was after play and I had fallen out with my friend and then I had to go to maths I would feel a bit upset, because other things happen before the maths, it's not just the maths that makes me happy or sad.

(Rhiannon, Avenue Primary, Year 6, bottom set)

Maths before lunch I'm not very good with because I am having bad lunchtimes and I have to go and tell Mr Iverson when I am feeling fine and when I am not. I normally like maths before break or after lunch, but not before lunch.

(Wynne, Avenue Primary, Year 4, bottom set)

Both Rhiannon and Wynne talked about the impact of broader events on their learning. Wynne's classteacher, Mr Iverson, was aware of the difficulties she was facing in maintaining positive peer relationships, yet was unable to give consistent pastoral support because Wynne was extracted from his care for mathematics and they were not in contact at key moments of the day such as before lunchtimes.

In addition to school-based events, a primary teacher's pastoral role includes being aware of how children's wider lives impact on their learning. However, there may be limited time for classteachers to share this information with set teachers, or limited capacity for set teachers to hold and respond to such information. At Avenue Primary, one child, Yolanda, was often late for mathematics and appeared disengaged. Yolanda's set teacher attributed her disengagement to a lack of ability and Yolanda was often reprimanded for not paying attention. However, speaking to Yolanda's classteacher revealed a chaotic home-life, something Yolanda touched on when asked to draw and talk about what she thought about in mathematics lessons:

Discussing her picture, it was clear that while some mathematics was part of her thoughts (sums and partitioning), Yolanda was preoccupied with external events:

Sometimes I miss my mum and my brother, it's just sometimes that pops into my head in maths because my brother is quite cute and my mum always gives me cuddles. I miss that. Sometimes I think about sums in maths.

(Yolanda, Avenue Primary, Year 4, bottom set)

The limited opportunity for the set teacher to engage with children beyond the mathematics teaching meant that the significant role of Yolanda's home-life was ostensibly, although unintentionally, ignored. The breakdown of pastoral support, as a hidden consequence of setting, may have contributed towards more negative impressions being formed of children and may have restricted learning opportunities as set teachers, working under a fixed-ability mindset, see a lack of ability rather than children facing external barriers to learning.

Subject teachers or primary teachers?

When a teacher teaches a set rather than their own class a shift occurs from a holistic to a subject-based focus. Children move to a set for a subject with a teacher who they may only encounter in the context of that subject. While classteachers develop a knowledge of their children that encompasses the whole school day, set teachers only know children in a subject-specific context. Although the set teacher's understanding of the child in that subject may be strong, they are limited in understanding children across the curriculum.

Within this study teachers were asked about the differences between teaching mathematics as a class-subject and when set:

Well it's, I don't know, it's got more, they're your children, they're your class and you know where they are across the curriculum and you know, I think that in itself can help me to understand, you know where to push them on a little bit more, but if you see them for an hour every day it's just more difficult.

(Mr Donaldson, Parkview Primary, Year 4 classteacher)

Mr Donaldson taught a Year 4 mixed-ability class for all subjects at Parkview Primary. Previously he taught in schools using setting and so was able to contrast his experiences of teaching within both structures. Mr Donaldson acknowledged the difficulties associated with setting whereby he felt there were restricted opportunities to engage fully with each child across the curriculum.

Mr Donaldson also talks about being better positioned to support children's learning when he sees them across the curriculum. This reflects a traditional primary school approach which responds flexibly to children's needs, drawing on children's ideas and imaginations. Often primary teachers will thread a theme across curricular areas helping children to make connections and utilising their interests to sustain engagement. Where setting splits the day into subjects, these opportunities are diminished. This was illustrated when talking to Zackary. Zackary was asked what he thought about in mathematics lessons and he provided a fairly standard answer rooted in school mathematics:

What is the answer and how to get there.

However, this is where the school mathematics ended, as Zackary continued unprompted:

And then there's this. I think about this all the time.

At this point, Zackary became engrossed in drawing an image of a robotic dinosaur, *Pleo*, enthusiastically expressing details of its development:

It's not my best drawing; it's got a bit mixed up. It's a robot and it's in the [shop] catalogue and it's called Pleo and it costs £250 but I'm still going to get it and I really really want it and it's going to be my biggest Christmas present ever and I'm only going to get that for Christmas and that's it. I'm thinking about it all the time, when I'm going to bed, when I get up in the morning. I think more about that than the maths. It's the most lifelike robot that anyone has ever made in the world. It makes noises, it interacts with you and it is exactly the same size as a baby komodo dragon. An adult komodo is about from the ceiling to down there and from about there to there but a baby would be about that and that's the size it would be. It took four years to make because they had to make the head the right size, but if they make it bigger that would increase the power but then in the motor there they would have to put more power in there and that would affect the leg power and that would affect the tail power. They had to work for four whole years, that's a very long time. I don't know if there will be a delay because it was supposed to come out in September but there was something wrong with its charger because it needs to be charged for eight hours.

(Zackary, Avenue Primary, Year 4, bottom set)

Zackary engages with some quite complex mathematical ideas involving ratio and proportion, time, and measurement, using ideas and quantities in excess of the one and two digit, manipulative-supported calculations that he was involved in in his bottom set mathematics lessons. However, in thinking about this dinosaur rather than engaging with the school mathematics, Zackary was constructed by his mathematics teacher as disengaged and of low mathematical ability. Had Zackary been taught by his classteacher there may have been the opportunity to elicit his interest and use it across the curriculum – using the dinosaur as a context for writing, mathematics, or design work – with the potential to engage Zackary and present a very different construction of him as a learner. There is of course no guarantee that this would happen as teachers work to balance the interests of children across their class, but setting represents a very real barrier to utilising a cross-curricular approach.

Ability-grouping and resource allocation

Chapter 5 examined some of the difficult choices schools and teachers face when, under a market-driven education system, they must make decisions about the allocation of limited resources. Schools strategically place resources, including teachers, in order to maximise outcomes. The link between ability-grouping and resource allocation may be even more deeply embedded than this suggests.

Teacher allocation

The creation of more sets than classes at Avenue Primary resulted in logistical issues in terms of staffing. With only three Year 6 teachers, a regular Year 6 teacher was not available for all sets. With the *best* teachers assigned to Set 1 and Set 3 (see Chapter 5) and the mathematics subject co-ordinator taking Set 2, the teaching of the bottom set was shared between Mr Leverton, a floating supply teacher, for three lessons a week, and a higher level teaching assistant (HLTA) for two lessons a week. Mr Leverton talked at length about his concern that he had seen in all year groups at Avenue Primary and across other primary schools the lowest sets being allocated the weakest or newest teachers or working with a teaching assistant:

I mean depending on the teachers that you have, if you've got a good range of teachers and you give your top set to a teacher who's really very good at it, then you are going to get a difference, but it depends on how you, sometimes the bottom set is often given to someone who has just come in I imagine, in some schools, the bottom set has a higher level teaching assistant taking them which I think is atrocious, I mean there, it's like if you've got dyslexia and you are given a teaching assistant to work with you but if you took it as a medical thing then you've got pneumonia and you're given a non-specialist nurse to look after you. If you've got something seriously wrong with you then you need a complete specialist to look after you, that's why if you have got dyslexia you should have an expert to look after you and not someone who is making it up and using games.

(Mr Leverton, Avenue Primary teacher)

Mr Leverton's concern about non-specialist teaching assistants being responsible for children with the greatest needs is born out in the literature (Webster et al, 2011). Schools allocate the strongest teachers to the top or high-stakes sets, reducing opportunities for children in bottom sets to develop any level of meaningful engagement with the subject, and potentially reproducing their non-mathematical low-ability identities. These practices reflect the US literature which suggests that:

Teacher tracking exacerbates the inequalities in opportunity to learn produced by tracking by matching the teachers who are most likely to be successful in the classroom with the students who already occupy a privileged position in the educational system.

(Kelly, 2009, p 454)

In effect, some children are doubly disadvantaged as a result of differentiated grouping practices and the tracking of their teachers.

Learning spaces

All ability-grouping involves some reorganisation and allocation of space. While primary school learning environments are under-theorised it is important to recognise that children's responses to the learning environment play a pivotal role in shaping their learner identity (Bibby et al, 2007). Individuals are changed by their experiences in particular spaces and different learning spaces 'can directly support or inhibit learning' (Clark, 2002, p 9).

At Avenue Primary, in common with many primary schools, creating more mathematics sets than classrooms left the bottom sets without stable learning bases. At the beginning of each mathematics lesson, these children were visible in not having a classroom to go to. Teachers had to find a learning space each day, walking around the school, carrying equipment and with their set trailing behind them. Spaces used included infant (ages 3–7) classrooms, special needs bases, PortaKabins and corridors. Children tried to rationalise these placements:

If we're in a different maths group that has to go in a different place we go in that classroom but sometimes we go in the science area or 3A, because, well, 4J, that's our maths teacher's classroom and so we just go in there but I don't really know why and sometimes Mr Hockins' maths group goes in Mrs Jerrett's room and so we go to the science and computer area but then Year 3 have computer time so we go into 3A.

(Wynne, Avenue Primary, Year 4, bottom set)

You know we're not normally in the classroom we were in today. Sometimes we go round there in the science area or sometimes we just go in the corridor, because in our classroom, usually someone else has Mrs Jerrett's classroom, we only go in Wednesday and Thursday in the classroom, the other days we go to like the science area.

(Zackary, Avenue Primary, Year 4, bottom set)

Wynne and Zackary show how complex these movements are, highlighting a lack of stability. There is a sense that these children did not fully understand their displacement, but saw others (in this case, children in higher sets) as having greater precedence over appropriate learning spaces.

Many of the spaces used by the bottom sets were physically located away from their year-group classrooms, requiring children to walk through early years and Key Stage 1 corridors. On some occasions, their presence in these areas was challenged by school staff, requiring the children to defend their spatial location, and possibly inciting feelings of exclusion. The use of these spaces took time away from teaching – in walking around the school to find an empty room – and brought further consequences. Particularly for the oldest children, infant classrooms contained furniture too small to be comfortable. Other environments were not conducive to learning:

The learning resource base Set 4 often used was unavailable today. We wandered round the school trying to find somewhere else to have the lesson for five to ten minutes. The lesson was conducted in a dusty cramped PortaKabin in the corner of the playground. Half the room was filled with old furniture. The sun was streaming into the unventilated PortaKabin and it quickly became very hot. I found it a very uncomfortable environment to work in and I suspect the children did too as they quickly removed sweaters and repeatedly asked for drinks or made excuses to leave the room, with most requests denied. The children were supposed to be working on individual worksheets on basic number fact recall (12+7, 3x4 etc) but these did not sustain their attention.

(Author's research notes, Avenue Primary, Year 6, bottom set)

Strikingly, this is not a one-off incident. Talking to teachers across the country reveals similar space allocations, particularly teaching in corridors, and a recent study from the United States reveals something very similar:

During my first semester, I taught English classes in the print shop. My next room turned out not to be a classroom at all. My students had nowhere to sit, and one of the kids said, 'Mr Alvarez, they always give you the cheap classrooms.' She sure was right. Finally, with 10 weeks to go in the year I was moved into a [third] room ... with one window that does not open, no air conditioner, and only one door to let in air. It has been close to 90 degrees every day. The students are being cheated out of a quality education ... I look at all the classes that have to endure this environment, and I see they all have one thing in common: they are lower-track classes. The four teachers who were in the print shop and now in the windowless bungalows for the most part have '103' students ... The school decided that the kids who need the most attention, the most help, should get the worst environment in which to learn. There is no way that the school would put honors kids in these rooms.

(Anderson and Oakes, 2014, p 117)

Such space allocations, a direct implication of ability-grouping practices, impact on children's learning:

In our group we could have done more get up and do except in that computer room there isn't a lot of space and you know in the corridor you're a bit constrained and a bit public as well because everyone is walking through.

(Mrs Jerrett, Avenue Primary, Year 4, bottom set teacher)

Mrs Jerrett highlights hidden implications of the space allocation related to ability-grouping. She notes restrictions on the types of activities that can be undertaken, with limited space to engage in anything other than seated work. Further, she suggests how lessons conducted in the corridor were not only disrupted by others walking through but also put the children on view to the rest of the school.

The lack of a consistent teaching space also had implications for access to mathematical and learning resources. It was not uncommon to hear teachers of bottom sets at Avenue Primary comment 'now I wonder where that is in this room' and in many cases teaching was limited by what the teacher could physically carry. Many teaching spaces used did not have interactive white boards, 100-squares and number lines commonly found in primary classrooms, limiting more spontaneous teaching. While comical to watch, children being forced to using metre-sticks instead of 30cm rulers (and poking their peers in the process) to draw tables in their books because their learning space lacked the most basic of classroom equipment carries implications for their learning and potentially for their sense of self-worth.

The implications of space allocation were not limited to the lowest sets. Due to unequal set sizes, high-ability sets often found themselves in groups larger than classrooms were intended to hold, with, for example, 35 children in the top set in Year 6 at Parkview Primary being taught in a classroom usually containing 28 children. This resulted in disruption at the beginning of lessons, finding chairs and physically fitting extra bodies and furniture in the room. As with finding a classroom for the lowest sets, this took time away from learning. Further, a number of children found themselves sat where their view of the whiteboard or teacher was restricted, again carrying implications for learning. As with the lowest sets in the corridor, teachers were restricted in the teaching methods they could employ with the physical space limiting activities to seated work.

IN A **NUTSHELL**

This chapter has examined some of the nuanced impacts of ability-grouping in primary schools, moving beyond the usual considerations of group allocation, attainment and attitude. Setting attempts to introduce a structure from secondary education, grounded in individual subjects, into the primary environment, usually grounded in holistic learning. Primary aged children must assume the roles and responsibilities of secondary school pupils. They move around the school for different subjects, respond to different teachers and work with different peer groups. These are quite extensive demands to make of primary aged children, sometimes from the age of four. Primary schools are not physically suited to, nor are primary aged children socially mature enough to cope with, setting and the inevitable subject cultures, particularly where this significantly reduces pastoral input. In particular, those children who experience the most difficulties in school often face the most changes and inconsistencies as a consequence of ability-grouping practices. Chapter 7 explores some of the implications of this in more detail, looking at the impacts of ability-grouping on peer-relationships.

REFLECTIONS ON **CRITICAL ISSUES**

- *We often think about ability-grouping in terms of attainment and attitude, but the impacts in primary schools may be wider. Schools need to consider classroom, teacher and resource allocation, opportunities for cross-curricular work, and changes to the traditional ethos.*

- *Setting may be better suited to secondary schools. Primary schools may lack the space to teach in sets, resulting in diminished learning environments for some children.*

- *Between-class grouping takes young children away from a stable classroom base, impacting on the holistic understanding of children and the pastoral role enacted by primary school teachers.*

CRITICAL **ISSUES**

- *To what extent are children aware of any differences between ability groups?*
- *Do all children experience placement in ability groups in the same ways?*
- *How might children's experiences impact their mathematics learning?*

Introduction

Chapter 4 examined children's understandings of ability and their self-labelling by group identifiers: a green person, a moped, or a 2A. Encountering the different treatments of different ability-groups, children produce stories to make sense of what is happening. This chapter explores how children experience, and make meaning from, the different teaching and learning approaches identified in Chapters 5 and 6.

Children's understandings of ability-grouping practices

Alongside children's identification with group labels emerged a strong awareness of the implications of the groups they were assigned to and an understanding that group labels carry significant meaning. Whether grouped within-class by recourse to colours, shapes or animals, or between classes with set numbers or by curriculum levels, children readily identified themselves and peers by group labels and understood the meanings of these:

All the 3Bs go to the side of us, the 3Cs go in the middle and the 2As, they go to the end.

(William, Riverside Primary, Year 4)

Children were aware that these positions meant something very particular, using a range of ability-predicated language (clever, good, best and worst) to, without hesitation, reel off the differences between children assigned to each group:

Mrs Ellery puts us into different groups, like maths groups … This means that you're good at maths, this means you are half at maths, the blue table means you don't have a clue.

(Kelly, Parkview Primary, Year 4)

Different experiences

Children showed awareness that the group they were assigned to had implications for the work they received. They were very quick to pick up on the differences, rehearsing, in particular, the belief that '*low-ability*' children could only cope with small numbers, despite this making the underlying mathematics no less complex:

Abbie: Same work but a bit easier, easier questions.

Ben: Yeah, maybe a one method question instead of a two method question.

Abbie: And easier numbers. Instead of thousands maybe using hundreds. Like if we have to times a number in the thousands by a number in the thousands, they might do a number in the hundreds by a number in the tens. The same thing but with smaller numbers.

(Parkview Primary, Year 6, top set)

Children were also aware of differential treatment. They identified that teachers directed questions at targeted individuals expected to get the questions right with the intention, particularly in top sets, of maintaining a fast pace. Astutely, both Uma and Peter below note that one implication of this may be that some children – Peter identifies these children as individuals in bottom groups – are not given a chance to become involved in the lesson or demonstrate their attainment. As illustrated later with Samuel in looking at bottom set experiences, not having the opportunity to demonstrate attainment, and hence feeling trapped in low groups, is a recurring theme.

That's why the teacher doesn't, never, picks on Victoria. It's always Thomas? Thomas? Thomas? Thomas? And she might think, oh the teacher's never going to pick me, there's no point in saying what I want to say, but she never just gets a chance.

(Uma, Avenue Primary, Year 4, top set)

The teachers would pick them for every question, every hard question and go to the not so good people for the easy questions. If it was the person down here [bottom group] the teacher won't involve them in lessons. They could get better, but no one would know because the teacher wouldn't pick them, it would be very difficult for them to show they were better.

(Peter, Avenue Primary, Year 6, bottom set)

Children expressed a view that different treatments were unfair and had impacts beyond the lesson content, impacts which may not be recognised by teachers. When asked how they would arrange mathematics groups if given the choice, Jessica and Louise discussed how ability-grouping made them feel about themselves and others:

Jessica: It wouldn't be as groups and people wouldn't think oh I'm better than everyone else or I'm worse than everyone else and be sad, and people think that now, because they are on the top-table or the bottom-table or something.

Louise: It makes you know you're worst at maths.

Jessica: And that makes her think she's not very good at maths. And other people call me the maths queen which I don't like because it seems like showing off and being the teacher's best pet.

(Parkview Primary, Year 4)

Despite this, some children, possibly repeating justifications heard in the home environment or from teachers, identified the benefits of assignment to groups, in particular the possibility of working with others at the same level and allowing the teacher to respond to everyone's learning needs:

In class maths it's fun seeing each other, what they can do and trying to help them, but sometimes it's quite nice just working with your own ability knowing that you can do the things on your own because sometimes the people in the top group just have to help the people in the bottom two which means that you're just helping them instead of trying to improve your own ability.

(Natalie, Avenue Primary, Year 6, top set)

While it has been shown that it is possible to manage giving appropriate levels of work within a mixed-ability class and that the process of explaining work to a peer supports others' understanding, Natalie's rationale – that in mixed-ability classes the high-ability children spend their time helping others – is one of the most common arguments put forward for the need for ability-grouping. Other children did put forward the alternative argument, namely that in mixed-ability classes children are able to support each other, benefit from a broader dialogue, and do not face the labelling implications of groups:

The clever people are spread out so that these people, if they don't know how to do it, they've got clever people on both sides of them so they can hear both people and just ask them.

(Jessica, Parkview Primary, Year 4)

The thing with class maths is that your friends know how thick, let's not say thick, but how like bad or how good are you, but if you come up to a group, like it's us four, five, so if we say something the other person will laugh and say ha-ha you got it wrong, but when you're in class your friends will be like hang on it doesn't matter let's give him another chance because we know he can do it, that's the best things about class maths, that and your mates can help you.

(Samuel, Avenue Primary, Year 6, bottom set)

Sam highlights the important role of friendship for a primary school child. Just as ability-grouping breaks down aspects of the traditional ethos of primary schooling, it also separates many children from friendship groups formed within classes:

You know in the groups? It takes you away from your friends, and sometimes it's like boys and one girl.

(Louise, Parkview Primary, Year 4)

Louise also noted how the gender imbalance in sets may contribute to difficulties in children establishing relationships in their new groups; relationships that it could be argued would be difficult to establish in any case given that these children only came together for an hour each day. Limited peer bonds in the new groups may impact on the success of collaborative working, although, as noted in Chapter 5, this was generally limited in many mathematics lessons.

Experiencing top sets: *it's like a zoo*

Weaker peer relationships from re-grouping alongside the fast-paced nature of top sets and a focus on answers results in a highly competitive environment – undoubtedly intensified by secondary selection practices – where children work for themselves. Where children did seek support from others, this was often denied:

Olivia: If you say I'm stuck on this one they're like oh my god that's easy but they don't help you or anything they carry on with what they are doing because it's almost like, for them, a race.

Megan: Yeah to finish first.

Olivia: And Miss Gundry always gives them loads of praise and a team point, like this morning I asked Matthew how to work something out and he's like just, you just multiply it, and I'm thinking great, that's really helpful.

(Avenue Primary, Year 6, top set)

The sarcasm in Olivia's comment speaks volumes for her interpretation of the unhelpful support given by Matthew as he seeks to maintain a focus on the completion of his work. Matthew, as with many children in top sets, rejected giving peer support in favour of finishing his work and completing more than others. Importantly, as Olivia attests to, these behaviours appear to be supported by the teacher in her award of merit marks to children overtly engaging in the race. Reward comes from self-focus rather than peer engagement.

The role of the teacher in maintaining the culture of the top sets was seen in the use and distribution of praise. A key feature of top set identity is correctness and not being wrong. Many children noted that praise was limited in top sets, with an expectation that they would always obtain full marks, resulting in what would usually be deemed a high standard of work being deemed as lacking in some way:

If you go down, even if you've done really well, so if you had 20 and then you get 18, you wouldn't get anything [ie a merit award] *even though you have still done well, which is quite upsetting for the task as you have still tried your hardest.*

(Natalie, Avenue Primary, Year 6, top set)

Such distribution of praise contributed to a top set culture where getting things wrong was viewed negatively and as something to be avoided rather than as an opportunity for improvement. This was played out in the behaviours of some children in the top set; behaviours that in many circumstances would be thought of as inappropriate but which were sanctioned within the top set culture:

Megan: I think it's more embarrassing for the people who are, who know, who are good at maths and they get something wrong, like today because Martha was doing the maths the other way she got the answer wrong and because she's quite good at maths the class were going ooohhh and boooo.

Olivia: Yeah and like, especially if you get an answer wrong then everyone shouts no, no, no and they go yes yes yes, it's quite like, it's like a zoo in the classroom it's terrible.

Megan: Yeah if you get an answer wrong everyone goes nooooo, it's this, and everyone goes, yeahhhhh.

(Avenue Primary, Year 6, top set)

Likening the top set classroom to a zoo may seem melodramatic but it does epitomise some of the quite extreme behaviours witnessed in these groups. It should be noted however that this was not an issue of classroom management and the same teachers were viewed responding very differently with their main classes or other groups of children where such behaviours would not be allowed. This was about the teacher and children co-constructing a very particular top set culture where children had to be correct and where mocking, rather than supporting, peers was essentially encouraged. The following case study examines some of the consequences for some children's learning that may arise from being within a potentially humiliating environment.

Girls and top sets: Megan's story – a case study

The embarrassment noted by Megan was felt particularly acutely by girls within the top sets and there was a sense that many girls – already outnumbered – felt inferior to the boys in their group:

I think the majority of boys in our group are better at maths than girls. There are no bad girls, but there are really really really good boys.

(Olivia, Avenue Primary, Year 6, top set)

Megan's story helps us understand how the culture of top sets may impact on learning. Despite being high-achieving and in the top set, Megan was an enigma to her teachers and peers. Although describing her as a gifted mathematician, they felt there was something about her classroom behaviour that set her apart from other high-achievers:

I think Megan is quite strange because most of the people who are really good in our group, they're always making sure that they get noticed and everything, but Megan keeps it to herself a bit more.

(Natalie, Avenue Primary, Year 6, top set)

Megan's classroom behaviours set her outside of the most able mathematicians in the top set, a group consisting predominantly of boisterous boys. While this group of boys did everything to ensure they were noticed – some behaviours being those that led Olivia to liken the set to a zoo – Megan appeared introverted. She rarely volunteered answers in class, was never observed asking questions and appeared to withdraw from lessons. The outward behaviours accompanying Megan's reluctance to participate in mathematics lessons were evidence used by her teachers in their later labelling of her as not one of the most able mathematicians in the set. Quite logically, they formed the opinion that she was not as quick as other children in obtaining answers and that in some cases she was unable to obtain answers other children achieved with ease.

It would be fairly simple to interpret Megan's actions and reactions at face-value. However, there was something far stronger underlying these. Close observation revealed that, far from not getting the answers quickly as her teachers assumed, Megan consistently produced fast correct answers. However, unlike those considered most able who shouted out and drew attention to themselves, she discretely wrote these down on her paper or whiteboard, keeping them to herself. Talking to Megan exposed the chasm between her outward observable behaviours and the feelings she was struggling to manage in the mathematics classroom:

If you are quite clever in some way, sometimes you don't want to get something wrong because other people might say something about that, so I would rather not say anything.

(Megan, Avenue Primary, Year 6, top set)

Megan was obtaining accurate answers quickly, but the top set culture of speed and correctness brought about a high level of anxiety. This led to her being fearful of making mistakes and as a result she made a decision not to participate, for as she says, she *'would rather not say anything'* than risk making a mistake and face humiliation from her peers in the zoo-like environment of the top set. Megan's strategy had serious implications for her learning of mathematics. She rarely took a risk and had limited opportunity to learn through her errors. Her teacher attributed her behaviours to something internal to Megan rather than a product of the top set culture. While Megan started from a high academic position at the beginning of Year 6, over the course of the year she made a gain in mathematics of just six months. Her hidden responses in class suggested that she should have achieved more than this. However, Megan's behaviours, stemming from heightened levels of anxiety, limited her in terms of the forms of participation required for success in a top set environment.

Megan's story is not unique. Her experiences mirror those of many top set girls in Boaler's (1997a) secondary mathematics study. Boaler found that while many boys in top sets were able to form goals related to speed, girls, valuing understanding, struggled to align with the top set culture, citing the teaching approach, pace and pressure of the top set as reasons for disaffection. Boaler also highlighted the anxiety felt by top set girls, importantly locating this within the school system and not as a deficit within particular pupils:

The girls at Amber Hill talked openly about their mathematical anxiety, but they did not attribute this anxiety to any deficiencies of their own. They were quite clear about the reason for their anxiety which was the system of school mathematics that they had experienced.

(Boaler, 1997a, p 119)

In a different environment Megan might have behaved in different ways. In interpreting her behaviours, Megan's teachers did not have access to her thoughts and anxieties and did not notice her quiet disaffection as she experienced an inability to align with the top set culture carrying with it implications for her mathematics engagement and learning both now and in the future.

Experiencing bottom sets: *my friends think I'm dumb*

Bottom set placement also brought particular experiences and possible limitations to learning. As discussed in Chapter 5, a feature of bottom sets is the strong behavioural focus and the amount of time spent by the teacher in behavioural interactions. This did not go unnoticed by the children who brought this up when asked about the differences between the sets, focussing predominantly on what they saw as the over strict and controlling behaviour of the teacher rather than any focus on mathematical issues. Importantly, as with the allowed behaviours in the top set, the children suggested that the same teachers interacted very differently with the children in other (non-set) lessons.

As a result of the teacher's perceived need to avoid behavioural issues, peer discussion and interaction was limited with children working on individualised tasks. An example was seen in the teacher's reaction to the boys' talk in the division task case study in Chapter 5, and Samuel explained how the teacher's view that any noise must be negative removed the possibility of supportive peer discussion:

I don't really know, he thinks me and Saul are like always bad, but we're not sometimes bad, like if I get stuck on a question I ask him, Saul, what's this, and he'll think we're talking, he doesn't even let us speak, we say 'he's trying to help me', but he doesn't let us speak.

(Samuel, Avenue Primary, Year 6, bottom set)

Samuel went on to explain how other features of the bottom set – particularly the small number of children – restricted dialogue and interaction and the pool of experiences children brought to the group, subsequently impacting on the learning of those children who experienced limited possibilities for learning from peers:

When you're in the other class, your class, you get to see your mates every day and with them, they can help you, and it's a bigger group and if you don't know the answer, you can ask anyone and they will help you out, but if you are in a group, hardly anyone, like if I say 'what's this answer' no one can help.

(Samuel, Avenue Primary, Year 6, bottom set)

This fits strongly with the earlier discussion where the importance of friendship groups and feeling comfortable with those you were working with was raised by a number of children. Samuel's quotations show how multiple factors, some intended to be supportive (such as small group sizes) and others related to assumptions around ability (such as the need for high levels of behavioural control) come together to put real barriers in the way of collaborative working and peer discussion, limiting the ways of working and mathematical experiences available to these children.

For Samuel, other factors related to his bottom set placement also came together to limit his learning experience. The low-levelness of the tasks set and Samuel's disapplication from the national tests – intended as a supportive action by the teachers – were viewed and experienced very differently by Samuel and his peers, limiting opportunities for Samuel to progress mathematically. Without being given access to higher-level work, without being given the opportunity to engage in mathematical discussion, and being disapplied from standardised testing, Samuel was never given the opportunity to make or show any improvement, something he was very aware of:

It makes me annoyed and sad and upset because I wanted to be top of the maths group, I always wanted to be when I was first into this school, but my wish didn't come true, I've always been last in every maths group … I'll just be low now in my next school too … Well I wanted to move, I wanted to move up, I wanted to move to up there, but I'm always there. I can't move even when I want to … the teachers say I can't do the test and my friends think I'm dumb for not being allowed to do the test. That's how it works, I won't do the test, it makes me unhappy and I can't get better to get the tests to go up.

(Samuel, Avenue Primary, Year 6, bottom set)

Samuel appears not to have accepted his position not because he believes it to be a true reflection of his achievement but because, despite trying to fight against the ability structures, he has been unable to move due to the practices surrounding his deterministic placement. He often talked about wanting to be in a higher set. While it could be argued that this was unrealistic, his assessment that, under present conditions, he *'can't get better'* seems accurate. Samuel's experiences mirror the findings of secondary pupils in Boaler's (1997a) lower sets who reported that restrictions arising as a result of set placement and teacher belief led to disaffection and underachievement. Much like Samuel reports, secondary mathematics *'students believed that they had been restricted, unfairly and harmfully, by their placement into sets'* (Boaler, 1997a, p 134). Other children across bottom sets reported similar restrictions to their learning and while many of these experiences arose from the teacher attempting to act in a supportive role, many consequences for children's opportunities to learn, and subsequently their levels of disaffection within mathematics, went unnoticed or misinterpreted as an aspect of their character rather than a reaction to the restrictions of their set placement.

IN A **NUTSHELL**

Children, mirroring wider educational and social discourse, use beliefs about ability to rationalise group placements and differential treatment. They are aware that different groups receive different experiences, in many cases suggesting that these differences are unfair, either for themselves or others. While a few children in top sets could identify some of the riches to be accrued from their placement, many children experienced ability-grouping as a rupturing of established within-class friendship groups with resultant difficulties establishing collaborative working with new peers in their ability-groups.

Children in top and bottom sets have, on the surface, very different experiences, yet there are similarities particularly in terms of, often hidden, implications. Children in all sets may be held back, experiencing restrictions on their mathematical learning opportunities either due to the competitive, self-absorbed culture of the top set or the extensive behavioural controls of the bottom set. Children in top sets feared making mistakes while those in bottom sets were not allowed access to mathematics beyond their perceived level. Although some implications of ability-grouping can be observed, the children's stories reveal that groups are being experienced in unexpected ways. Outward behaviours may be misinterpreted and wrongly ascribed to some internal quality of the child: a linkage made altogether easier through strong fixed-ability beliefs.

REFLECTIONS ON **CRITICAL ISSUES**

- *Children can easily explain differences between groups in terms of common ability language and are acutely aware that differently labelled groups receive different treatment.*

- *Children have different experiences across groups. Within groups, some children – such as high-achieving girls – may experience aspects of the set culture differently or more acutely.*

- *Although experiences are different, the impacts for many children, often in terms of restricted mathematical learning opportunities, are remarkably similar.*

Introduction

This book has linked theory with policy and practice in a critical examination of ability-thinking and practices in primary schools. The preceding chapters have discussed the history of ability-grouping practices – with a focus on the primary school where previous research has been more limited – and have examined why the language of ability is so prevalent within the English education system. Children's experiences – brought alive through their words – have been used to illustrate both the overt and more nuanced implications of the use of ability language and grouping in the primary classroom. Examples have predominantly been drawn from the mathematics classroom where ability-grouping in one form or another is relatively ubiquitous, but these findings can easily be transferred to the use of ability-grouping and ability-thinking across the primary school.

The findings presented across this book, in line with other research into ability-grouping, make it clear why it is fair to say that children's futures may be being dictated at the age of four – in Reception classes – and how organisational practices can create and exaggerate attainment differences between children. Boaler (2005) identified how setting structures in secondary mathematics create *psychological prisons*, limiting individuals' engagement with mathematics well beyond school. It appears that the primary school, also driven by assumptions of fixed-ability, while perhaps having less obvious prison walls, represents an extension of such constraint.

Within the context of a rapidly changing political and educational landscape, and recognising the incumbent pressures – internal and external – on teachers, this final chapter considers the challenges of change and the possibilities for a future where all children have access to an engaging and rewarding education.

Change in mathematical needs

Chapter 5 suggested that ability-grouping appears to be leading to a particular type of mathematics teaching and learning dominated by procedures and correct answers rather than sustained engagement with complex problems. Mathematics becomes an individual, rather than collaborative, endeavour. Mathematics is conceptualised only in a very formal sense. The mathematics that people engage with on a daily basis, often using ad hoc methods rather than formal algorithms, is not seen as real mathematics, leading to a somewhat bizarre situation where adults can simultaneously demonstrate mathematical fluency while claiming not to be good at mathematics:

I'm trying to do it equally into 12, so a little bit of maths, and maths isn't my strong point, so I'm going to do it into three first of all and then divide each three into quarters.

(Mat, *The Great British Bake Off*, BBC Television, 2 September 2015)

At its inception, mass schooling was developed to meet the needs of society within the industrial age, ensuring conformity to, and the reproduction of, social structures. Society, and the workplace, is now, on the whole, far more fluid and the mathematical needs of society have changed considerably. Repeatedly concerns are raised about the mathematical skills of school-leavers entering the workforce with attempts made to pin-down the mathematical skills sought by employers in the age of *big data* (The British Academy, 2015). Such concerns need to be taken seriously and we need to ensure the education children receive today will allow them to flourish in this new mathematical world. Unfortunately, the type of mathematics that comes with fixed-ability thinking has not moved on to match this new world, hence the urgent need now to consider avenues for change.

The challenge of fixed-ability thinking and practices

For forty years we have been too preoccupied with the mere measurement of ability; with testing and grading, with selection and rejection and allocation. Many teachers and administrators have almost come to regard this classification as their main job. Worshipping at an altar bearing the mystic symbol 'IQ', set up by a priesthood of pseudo-scientists called 'psychometrists', they have sometimes seemed to forget the age-old power of teaching, and the capacity of a child to keep on growing and learning – when it is put in the right environment.

(Pedley, 1963, p192)

Robin Pedley (1914–88) would, I suspect, be rather dismayed to find that what he said over 50 years ago spoke to the educational landscape today. We may not use the term IQ so directly (although it is barely camouflaged in, for example, the Cognitive Abilities Tests (CATs) taken in early secondary school) but replace this with ability – which Gillborn and Youdell (2000) refer to as *The new IQism* – and this statement succinctly outlines thinking across primary and secondary education. As noted in previous chapters, this thinking, and its associated practices, is deep-rooted and impervious to change. While remembering *the capacity of the child to keep on growing* underpins some quite recent alternatives to fixed-ability thinking, it is always going to be difficult to enact change in a culture still clinging to any remnants of classification, labelling and associated fixed-ability thinking. Further, classrooms are inherently complex places with an unpredictable interplay between the teacher, the curriculum and the class. Approaches that appear to work in one class may look very different in another class, even with the same teacher or curriculum (Even, 2014). As such, any alternative to current ways of thinking and working needs to engage with this complexity, allowing individual teachers to reflect on their beliefs and actions with their classes.

Is mixed-ability teaching a viable alternative?

It is common to hear individual teachers or schools stating that they have moved towards mixed-ability teaching having had, perhaps, their assumptions about ability-grouping challenged or following a wider school concern for equity. This is, of course, to be commended. However, a little caution is needed. The term *mixed-ability* still implies some notion of, and reference to, *ability* with its inherent underlying assumptions. Abandoning ability-grouping practices or labels does not in itself eradicate ability-thinking. Fixed-ability thinking continues to pervade teaching and learning practices and teacher–child interactions even in mixed-ability environments. An ability discourse, even when used in apparently '*benign*' (Dixon et al, 2002, p 9) ways, and an ideologically driven tendency to think about individuals in terms of capacity and limits, continues to present itself, even outside of explicit grouping, in classroom practices. The following case study from a Year 4 mixed-ability class at Parkview Primary illustrates the need for caution.

Persistent fixed-ability assumptions – a case study

Mrs Ellery's class are working on problem-solving using multiplication. The children are working in pairs, and are all doing the same task. These pairs are generally ability-based as children are sitting on their mathematics tables.

The children have to choose 12 animals (eg six cats, four ducks and two spiders) and work out how many wellington boots the animals would need in total. The teacher goes through the task on the interactive white board showing the children how to work it out and complete the table before doing it themselves with their choice of animals.

A pair of children on the blue table (labelled by the teacher as the lowest ability) talk animatedly about the animals they are choosing, laughing that they are going to pick underwater animals without any legs so their answer will be zero. They choose five goldfish, five whales and two sharks. They write out the mathematics as they have been asked, to show that their animals require no wellingtons and get up excitedly to show what they have done to the teacher.

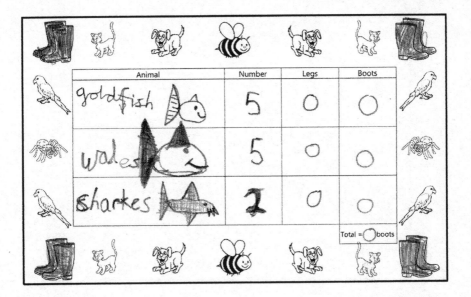

Animal	Number	Legs	Boots
goldfish	5	○	○
wales	5	○	○
sharkes	1	○	○
		Total = ○ boots	

The teacher looks very briefly at their work, tells them the table is untidy and their handwriting difficult to read before telling them off loudly in front of the class for not picking sensible animals and not doing the task properly. They are given a clean sheet and told to repeat the task correctly. The children return to their table but do no further mathematical work, instead talking and fiddling with classroom equipment.

Towards the end of the lesson, the teacher asks some children to share their work with the class. A pair from the green table (labelled by the teacher as the highest ability) goes to the front and shows their work to the class. Before looking at the mathematics they have done, the teacher praises them for completing the work so neatly saying that this makes the mathematics they have done easy to understand. The teacher then asks one of the pair to read out what they have written to the class while the other child completes the table on the interactive white board. The children's table includes:

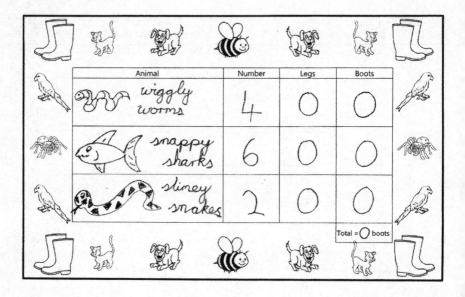

The teacher laughs along with the pair and the rest of the class, telling them they are very clever choosing animals with no legs. She praises the children for their good thinking.

Commentary on case study

This case study illustrates how teachers may respond differently to similar situations. This is an illuminating extract because these situations occur within the same lesson, with the same teacher, and within approximately 20 minutes of each other. It could reasonably be expected that when the teacher encountered the second situation she would still have some memory of the first. The first pair of children encountered a negative reference to non-mathematical aspects of their work and two behavioural reprimands audible to the class. The second pair of children encountered positive teacher engagement, reference to their neat work with some, albeit minimal, linkage made between this and a mathematical context, and praise encompassing words including *clever* and *good* which the rest of the class were encouraged to be a part of through sharing in the teacher instigated laughter.

It is not possible to say that the differences in the reaction of the teacher are entirely due to fixed-ability thinking and resultant assumptions about the work and behaviour of different children, yet this is potentially a relevant factor. The first pair of children – expected to perform a low-ability identity – break out of these expectations, performing aspects of a high-ability identity: working quickly, getting their work correct (the mathematics they completed was correct for the numbers chosen) and working with enthusiasm. These behaviours are reconstructed by the teacher, realigning the children with their low-ability identity. Rather than acknowledge that they have worked quickly, their work is referred to as difficult to read. This comment, highlighting common value-judgements about neatness in primary classrooms, ties in with, and strengthens, children's constructions of ability. The second pair of children produced limited work in comparison to other children given the numbers chosen and the limited mathematics involved. They produced the same quantity of work in the lesson that the blue-table pair had completed 20 minutes earlier. However, the teacher makes no reference to this, instead focussing on positive aspects of the work, linking these to being mathematical and potentially strengthening a mathematical as opposed to behavioural identity for these children. It is possible that the teacher's construction of them as able fed into her construction of them as working mathematically. It is worth noting that while the teacher did not identify the first pair's work on multiplication by zero as mathematical, having time to think this through, and then having it re-presented to her by a perceived able pair, may have allowed her to reconstruct multiplication by zero as important and mathematical, rather than time-wasting and inappropriate.

This case study suggests that what is important is what is done – by teachers and others – within a structural organisation, as opposed to just the structural organisation. Seemingly innocuous interactions may be driven by notions of fixed-ability and stratified practices may appear so natural as to go undetected, even by the enactors, within the classroom. Change needs to go far deeper than a surface change to structural practices (switching to the use of mixed-ability teaching) or a change to the language (avoiding the term ability).

What are the alternatives?

While change is clearly both challenging and complex, we have multiple stories of hope including:

> » individuals resisting fixed-ability practices (Milik and Boylan, 2013);

> » teacher-training programmes challenging *bell-curve thinking* (Florian, 2013);

> » research projects engaging groups of teachers passionate about change (such as the Learning Without Limits (LWL) project, Hart et al, 2004);

> » jurisdictions where ability-grouping is rare or non-existent (such as in many Scandanavian countries including Finland, see for example Sahlberg, 2011).

Of course, as noted repeatedly, change cannot be surface level but must engage with teachers' core values and beliefs, particularly if any change is to be sustained. Our first challenge is to engage with the dominant social and educational discourse of fixed-ability underpinning so much of what is done in schools:

A spectre haunts social science: the spectre of the brain.

(Fitzgerald and Callard, 2015, p 3)

We might be encouraged that the lucrative industry of neuroscience fads recently infiltrated into classrooms seems to be waning as the neuro-mythologies on which these are built are rightly challenged (Snook, 2012). However, the wider *spectre of the brain*, of (pseudo) neuroscientific beliefs and actions, is still strong in schools, not least in fixed-ability thinking. Until this spectre is challenged, we face an uphill, if not impossible, struggle to bring about change.

Challenging teachers' core beliefs, to ask them to forego the *common sense* of ability-thinking, is a huge undertaking given so many of their practices will be built upon this. This change, essentially an identity shift, is not an easy one to undertake alone. Unfortunately, *alone* very much characterises how much teaching in primary schools in England takes place, an isolated profession where, except under the auspices of performance management, we rarely witness and discuss the teaching and learning in each other's classrooms:

My classroom is my castle, and the sovereigns of other fiefdoms are not welcome here.

(Palmer, 1998, p 142)

Given that ability-thinking is so strongly embedded both culturally and historically in the English education system and wider society, teachers need networks if they are not to feel alone. Seeing others grappling with the same issues and thinking and working in similar ways to themselves allows them to believe that they have the power to bring about change. Such change cannot be a technique or set of methods to impose on practice but must instead come from within teachers. The changes that need to occur are not directly to language or to practice but are to the principles guiding decisions about practices. This change in the underlying principles of practice is essentially a change of mindset, characterised by the *LWL* project as a change from an ability to a *transformability* mindset (Hart et al, 2004). Such change requires teachers to ask difficult questions about their beliefs and about what guides their practices. To ask teachers to engage with their guiding principles, with their mindset, and potentially to change this, requires them to have the time and space to reflect on what their principles currently are and the beliefs they hold about different ways of working:

A teacher without time to think is like an artist asked to paint without being able to stand back and look at the results of what she's doing. And when, in the end, she sees that her picture is a flop, she blames not her restricted space, her need to work very fast, her inability to stand back and take cogent squints at her latest brush strokes. No, she blames the canvas.

(Pye, 1988, p 174)

Many of the teachers whose voices appear in this book were considering these issues for the first time. The highly doctrinaire, prescriptive and accountability-driven educational culture currently prevalent in England is not one that really supports reflection – individual or collegial – or gives space to think, meaning practices may be enacted without thought for the underlying beliefs or the resultant consequences. The teachers in this book found that when given the space to consider the practices of ability-grouping they could not logically defend this other than through recourse to the way things had always been done. These teachers, involved in reproducing many of the same experiences they had as children, had never been given the space, time or resources to think through the pervasive ability-driven practices they engaged in, the policies they implemented or the implications of these for their class. Teachers need to be given the space and opportunities to critically engage with their practices. Unfortunately the collaborative thoughtful approaches to teaching practices documented in projects where change has been successful are scarce in many schools, not through the wrong-doings of the schools or teachers, but through a legacy of fixed-ability thinking which permeates not only schools, but society more broadly.

Given the above, trainees will encounter a confusing and often contradictory mix of theory (such as that presented in this book), national and local policy and the observation of fixed-ability language and practices on placement. Teacher educators need to give trainees the time and space to explore these tensions, to reflect on *normal* interactions and to identify underlying belief systems. This way, we have the opportunity to disrupt damaging fixed-ability mindsets from the start.

FINAL **REFLECTIONS**

We live in a world where ability-based labelling and stratification are the norm, not just in our schools but in wider society. We are bombarded with the language of ability, talent and intelligence to name but a few and it is little wonder that many people – including teachers, parents and children – assume that these messages and accompanying stratified practices must be correct and therefore that such views of human capacity continue to go unchallenged. This chapter asks the question: '*Should we just change the language?*' It seems clear, given how embedded this language is and how persistent practices related to this language are, that such a surface level change will do little to impact on the multiple implications of a discourse with such a strong history in our education system. It may be a start, but change needs to run far deeper.

Teachers are in a very difficult position, not only immersed in this ability-dominated world but also facing surveillance and external scrutiny both formally through inspections and appraisal and informally through the media. As such, change will be difficult, but there is evidence that this is not impossible. Change will involve challenging the deeply embedded layers of fixed-ability beliefs underscoring education in England. However the rewards of achieving such change hopefully outweigh the efforts of getting there; in the absence of fixed-ability thinking it is potentially possible to provide all children with access to an engaging and rewarding curriculum, one that encourages sustained collaborative working and the development of transferable problem-solving skills, rather than, as we currently have, one which only allows selected children to succeed.

If teachers were given the space and the time to engage with the practices that have become so normalised as to go unquestioned and if teacher educators were to find spaces to encourage trainees to question inconsistencies between theory, policy and practice, we could develop a culture where reflection is the norm. Time out to reflect and partake in professional conversations could provide teachers with the time to think about their practice and that of others. Currently, teachers lead fairly individualised lives and the same ability-predicated practices and pressures which are detrimental to children may also place teachers in competition with each other. Giving time to explore what is happening may make them more reflective, thoughtful and essentially *better* teachers. This happens in other professions where professionals are taking on so much (eg therapeutic and medical settings) so why not in an educational context? To do so would require a sustained commitment to the pastoral care of teachers, giving them the opportunity to care for themselves as well as their children. Doing so, although contrary to much current practice in education, may enable them to see, to challenge, and ultimately to change, the reproductive and stigmatising processes they are involved in.

This book has uncovered practices and interactions taking place in the classroom that some teachers and trainees may find quite challenging particularly if they have engaged in these themselves without reflection on the underlying belief systems or on the philosophies underlying the policies they are asked to enact. Teacher educators have an important role to play here in encouraging their trainees to reflect on their beliefs and principles and on the key messages of this book. In this way, informed change can be promoted from the start of a trainee's career.

»   What impact have the stories in this book had on your beliefs and
    principles about teaching and learning?

»   How might engaging with this book change your classroom practice?

REFERENCES

Anderson, L and Oakes, J (2014) The Truth About Tracking, in Gorski, P and Zenkov, K (eds) *The Big Lies of School Reform: Finding Better Solutions for the Future of Public Education.* Abingdon, Oxon: Routledge.

Ball, S (1981) *Beachside Comprehensive.* Cambridge: Cambridge University Press.

Barker Lunn, J (1970) *Streaming in the Primary School: A Longitudinal Study of Children in Streamed and Non-Streamed Junior Schools.* Slough: National Foundation for Educational Research.

Bartholomew, H (1999) Setting in stone? How ability-grouping practices structure and constrain achievement in mathematics, paper presented at British Educational Research Association 25th annual conference, University of Sussex, September 1999.

BERA-RSA (2014) *Research and the Teaching Profession – Building Capacity for a Self-Improving Education System.* London: BERA. [online] Available at: bera.ac.uk.

Bibby, T, Moore, A, Clark, S and Haddon, A (2007) *Children's Learner-Identities in Mathematics at Key Stage 2: Final Report.* London: Institute of Education.

Boaler, J (2005) The 'Psychological Prisons' from Which They Never Escaped: The Role of Ability Grouping in Reproducing Social Class Inequalities. *Forum,* 47: 135–43.

Boaler, J (1997a) *Experiencing School Mathematics: Teaching Styles, Sex and Setting.* Buckingham: Open University Press.

Boaler, J (1997b) Setting, Social Class and Survival of the Quickest. *British Educational Research Journal,* 23: 575–95.

The British Academy (2015) *Count Us In: Quantitative Skills for a New Generation.* London: The British Academy.

Broadfoot, P, Osborn, M, Gilly, M and Paillet, A (1987) Teachers' Conceptions of their Professional Responsibility: Some International Comparisons. *Comparative Education,* 23: 287–301.

Campbell, T (2014) Stratified at Seven: In-class Ability Grouping and the Relative Age Effect. *British Educational Research Journal,* 40: 749–71.

Campbell, T (2015) How Stereotypes Reinforce Inequalities in Primary School. *The Conversation,* 15th June 2015. [online] Available at: www.theconversation.com/how-stereotypes-reinforce-inequalities-in-primary-school-43127 (accessed 7 October 2015).

Clark, H (2002) *Building Education: The Role of the Physical Environment in Enhancing Teaching and Research.* London: Institute of Education.

Davies, J, Hallam, S and Ireson, J (2003) Ability Groupings in the Primary School: Issues Arising from Practice. *Research Papers in Education,* 18: 45–60.

Department for Education (2008) School Performance Tables: Performance tables 1994–2012. [online] Available at: www.education.gov.uk/schools/performance/archive/index.shtml (accessed 7 October 2015).

Department for Education and Employment (1997) *Excellence in Schools.* London: HMSO.

Department for Education and Schools (2005) *Higher Standards, Better Schools for All: More Choice for Parents and Pupils.* London: Department for Education and Skills.

Department of Education and Science (1959) *Primary Education: Suggestions for the Consideration of Teachers and Others Concerned with the Work of Primary Schools.* London: Her Majesty's Stationery Office.

Dixon, A, Drummond, M J, Hart, S and McIntyre, D (2002) Developing Teaching Free from Ability Labelling: Back Where We Started? *Forum*, 44: 7–12.

Dweck, C (2012) *Mindset: How You Can Fulfil Your Potential*. New York: Ballantaine Books.

Education Endowment Fund (2015) Teaching and Learning Toolkit. [online] Available at: www. educationendowmentfoundation.org.uk/toolkit/toolkit-a-z/ (accessed 7 October 2015).

Even, R (2014) The Interplay of Factors Involved in Shaping Students' Opportunities to Learn Mathematics, in Li, Y, Silver, E and Li, S (eds) *Transforming Mathematics Instruction*. London: Springer.

Fitzgerald, D and Callard, F (2015) Social Science and Neuroscience Beyond Interdisciplinary: Experimental Entanglements. *Theory, Culture and Society*, 32: 3–32.

Florian, L (2013) Preparing Teachers to Work with *Everybody:* A Curricular Approach to the Reform of Teacher Education. *Forum*, 55: 95–102.

Friedrich, A, Flunger, B, Nagengast, B, Jonkmann, K and Trautwein, U (2015) Pygmalion Effects in the Classroom: Teacher Expectancy Effects on Students' Math Achievement. *Contemporary Educational Psychology*, 41: 1–12.

Gillborn, D and Youdell, D (2000) *Rationing Education: Policy, Practice, Reform and Equity*. Buckingham: Open University Press.

Gray, E and Tall, D (1994) Duality, Ambiguity, and Flexibility: A 'Proceptual' View of Simple Arithmetic. *Journal for Research in Mathematics Education*, 25: 116–40.

Hallam, S and Deathe, K (2002) Ability Grouping: Year Group Differences in Self-Concept and Attitudes of Secondary School Pupils. *Westminster Studies in Education*, 25: 7–17.

Hallam, S and Ireson, J (2005) Secondary School Teachers' Pedagogic Practices when Teaching Mixed and Structured Ability Classes. *Research Papers in Education*, 20: 3–24.

Hallam, S and Parsons, S (2013) Prevalence of Streaming in UK Primary Schools: Evidence from the Millennium Cohort Study. *British Educational Research Journal*, 39: 514–44.

Hallam, S and Parsons, S (2014) The Incidence and Make Up of Ability Grouped Sets in the UK Primary School. *Research Papers in Education*, 28: 393–420.

Hallam, S and Toutounji, I (1996) *What do We Know about the Grouping of Pupils by Ability?: A Research Review*. London: Institute of Education.

Hallam, S, Ireson, J and Davies, J (2004) Primary Pupils' Experiences of Different Types of Grouping in School. *British Educational Research Journal*, 30: 515–33.

Hallam, S, Ireson, J and Davies, J (2013) *Effective Pupil Grouping in the Primary School: A Practical Guide*. London: Routledge.

Hallam, S, Ireson, J, Lister, V, Chaudhury, I and Davies, J (2003) Ability Grouping Practices in the Primary School: A Survey. *Educational Studies*, 29: 69–83.

Hamilton, L (2002) Constructing Pupil Identity: Personhood and Ability. *British Educational Research Journal*, 28: 591–602.

Harlen, W and Malcolm, H (1999) *Setting and Streaming: A Research Review*. Edinburgh: The Scottish Council for Research in Education.

Hart, S, Dixon, A, Drummond, M J and McIntyre, D (2004) *Learning Without Limits*. Maidenhead: Open University Press.

Heisig, J and Solga, H (2015) Secondary Education Systems and the General Skills of Less- and Intermediate-Educated Adults: A Comparison of 18 Countries. *Sociology of Education*, 88: 202–25.

Howe, M (1996) Concepts of Ability, in Dennis, I and Tapsfield, P (eds) *Human Abilities: Their Nature and Measurement*. Mahwah, NJ: Lawrence Erlbaum Associates.

Howe, M (1997) *IQ in Question: The Truth about Intelligence.* London: SAGE.

Jackson, B (1964) *Streaming: An Educational System in Miniature.* London: Routledge and Kegan Paul.

Kelly, S (2009) Tracking Teachers, in Saha, L and Dworkin, A (eds) *International Handbook of Research on Teachers and Teaching.* New York: Springer.

Kulik, C and Kulik, J (1982) Research Synthesis on Ability Grouping. *Educational Leadership*, 39: 619–21.

Lacey, C (1970) *Hightown Grammar: The School as a Social System.* Manchester: Manchester University Press.

Lee, J and Croll, P (1995) Streaming and Subject Specialism at Key Stage 2: A Survey in Two Local Authorities. *Educational Studies*, 21: 155–65.

Marks, R (2013) 'The Blue Table Means You Don't Have a Clue': The Persistence of Fixed-Ability Thinking and Practices in Primary Mathematics in English Schools. *Forum*, 55: 31–44.

Marks, R (2014a) Educational Triage and Ability-Grouping in Primary Mathematics: A Case-Study of the Impacts on Low-Attaining Pupils. *Research in Mathematics Education*, 16: 38–53.

Marks, R (2014b) The Dinosaur in the Classroom: What We Stand to Lose Through Ability-Grouping in the Primary School. *Forum*, 56: 45–54.

Mcpherson, G (2015) 4-Year-Old Pupils Grouped by Ability. *Cambridge News*, 5 June 2015.

Milik, A and Boylan, M (2013) Valuing Choice as an Alternative to Fixed-ability Thinking and Teaching in Primary Mathematics. *Forum,* 55: 161–71.

Muijs, D and Dunne, M (2010) Setting by Ability – or Is It? A Quantitative Study of Determinants of Set Placement in English Secondary Schools. *Educational Research*, 52: 391–407.

Oakes, J (1982) The Reproduction of Inequity: The Content of Secondary School Tracking. *The Urban Review*, 14: 107–20.

Office for Standards in Education (1998) *Setting in Primary Schools.* London: Ofsted.

Palmer, P (1998) *The Courage to Teach: Exploring the Inner Landscape of a Teacher's Life.* San Francisco, CA: Jossey-Bass.

Parsons, S and Hallam, S (2014) The Impact of Streaming on Attainment at Age Seven: Evidence from the Millennium Cohort Study. *Oxford Review of Education*, 40: 567–89.

Pedder, D (2006) Are Small Classes Better? Understanding Relationships Between Class Size, Classroom Processes and Pupils' Learning. *Oxford Review of Education*, 32: 213–34.

Pedley, R (1963) *The Comprehensive School.* Harmondsworth: Penguin Books.

Povey, H (2010) Teaching for Equity, Teaching for Mathematical Engagement. *Philosophy of Mathematics Education Journal*, 25. [online] Available at: http://people.exeter.ac.uk/PErnest/pome25/index.html (accessed 7 October 2015).

Pye, J (1988) *Invisible Children: Who are the Real Losers at School?* Oxford: Oxford University Press.

Reay, D and Wiliam, D (1999) 'I'll be a Nothing': Structure, Agency and the Construction of Identity Through Assessment. *British Educational Research Journal*, 25: 343–54.

Rosenthal, R and Jacobson, L (1992) *Pygmalion in the Classroom: Teacher Expectation and Pupils' Intellectual Development.* Bancyfelin, Carmarthen: Crown House Publishing.

Sahlberg, P (2011) *Finnish Lessons.* New York: Teachers College Press.

Slavin, R (1987) Ability Grouping and Student Achievement in Elementary Schools: A Best-Evidence Synthesis. *Review of Educational Research*, 57: 293–336.

Snook, I (2012) Educational Neuroscience: A Plea for Radical Scepticism. *Educational Philosophy and Theory*, 44: 445–49.

Sternberg, R (1998) Abilities are Forms of Developing Expertise. *Educational Researcher*, 27: 11–20.

Stobart, G (2008) *Testing Times: The Uses and Abuses of Assessment*. London: Routledge.

Sukhnandan, L and Lee, B (1998) *Streaming, Setting and Grouping by Ability: A Review of the Literature*. Slough: National Foundation for Educational Research.

Syed, M (2011) *Bounce: The Myth of Talent and the Power of Practice*. New York: HarperCollins.

van Elk, R, van der Steeg, M and Webbink, D (2011) Does the Timing of Tracking Affect Higher Education Completion? *Economics of Education Review*, 30: 1009–21.

Webster, R, Blatchford, P, Bassett, P, Brown, P, Martin, C and Russell, A (2011) The Wider Pedagogical Role of Teaching Assistants. *School Leadership and Management*, 31: 3–20.

Whitburn, J (2001) Effective Classroom Organisation in Primary Schools: Mathematics. *Oxford Review of Education*, 27: 411–28.

Wiliam, D and Bartholomew, H (2004) It's not Which School but Which Set You're in that Matters: The Influence of Ability Grouping Practices on Student Progress in Mathematics. *British Educational Research Journal*, 30: 279–93.

Wilkinson, S and Penney, D (2014) The Effects of Setting on Classroom Teaching and Student Learning in Mainstream Mathematics, English and Science Lessons: A Critical Review of the Literature in England. *Educational Review*, 66: 411–27.

Wintour, P (2015) Labour Must Do More to Cater for Gifted Children, Says Tristram Hunt. *The Guardian*, Monday 2 March 2015. [online] Available at: www.theguardian.com/politics/2015/mar/02/labour-help-gifted-children-tristram-hunt (accessed 7 October 2015).

INDEX